Turning the Pages

Robert Brouwer

Turning
the Pages

Recollections of a musical autograph
collector and page-turner at the
Amsterdam Concertgebouw

Kahn & Averill
London

First published in 2003 by
Kahn & Averill
9 Harrington Road, London SW7 3ES

British Library Cataloguing in Publication Data
A catalogue record for this book is available from the British Library

ISBN 1-871082-80-3

Set in Monotype Joanna and designed by Simon Stern
Printed in Great Britain by
Halstan & Co Ltd, Amersham, Bucks

To Mon, my dear wife - the only episode of my life she did not share.

Contents

Preface

I can safely say that music has been the unbroken thread throughout my now fairly long life. It is fascinating to observe a work changing through the prisma of ageing over a period of more than sixty years and yet at the same time still remain the same. Occasionally one comes full circle. I heard Mozart's *Marriage of Figaro* for the first time in Amsterdam at the age of sixteen with a famous cast under Bruno Walter and with the Concertgebouw Orchestra in the pit. I heard it again recently at the age of eighty at the Theater an der Wien in Vienna with a young cast and the Vienna Philharmonic under Ricardo Muti, and the impression was as fresh as the first time.

I can give the reader a clue about what prompted me to write this rather light-hearted volume about performing musicians. Throughout my life they have been in the service of music which, as Artur Schnabel put it, "is better than can be performed". Witnessing the transfiguration of performers on and off the platform is an absorbing experience. Musicians leave one world and enter another, to return after what sometimes seems an eternity, but is actually no more than a few hours. I realize now that the privilege of witnessing this transformation at close range is one of the reasons which initially drove me to page turning and later to seek the company of the performers. Once the concert is over this spell is broken, but a special relationship continues and can be very rewarding. This is what these stories are about.

I should like to express my sincere gratitude to the many people who generously gave their help before and during the birth of this book, out of interest in its subject. The first impulse came from George Loudon – my old, though much younger friend and fellow Dutch expatriate, who lives in London. During a joint visit to Berlin in 1998 I found myself unexpectedly telling stories from my distant youth to George and his charming wife Angie. Suddenly Angie said "These stories are unique. You should write

them down!" I thought this was her polite way of saying "This is a bore. Shut up!" but a few weeks later the phone rang and it was George saying they had been serious and that he knew a young lady in Oxford willing to help me. This was Rosamund Bartlett, a lecturer and writer on Russian music and literature, with experience in publishing. Then and there the die was cast. Rosamund transcribed my tapes, became my editor and a dear friend, and saw the project through to fruition. Without George and Rosamund I would not even have made this effort.

Then there is my friend of 67 years, Theo Olof, who made a splendid career on the concert podium and as concertmaster of the Concertgebouw Orchestra. Not only did he agree at once to write a Foreword, he was also the invaluable go-between when I found it difficult to establish certain contacts.

My next help and encouragement came from Tully Potter, editor of Classic Record Collector. He critically read the manuscript and was the inexhaustible source of most of the photographs from his invaluable private collection. I am much indebted to him.

Paul Op de Coul, a more recent friend, is Professor of Musicology at the University of Utrecht, and provided a number of factual corrections. Paul is of a younger generation and it was very encouraging to know that he found my project worthwhile.

With Wolfgang Steinmayer, the well-known caricaturist, whose work I saw during a Schubertiade in Feldkirch, Austria, I developed a brief but cordial relationship, the result of which was the drawing which appears on the back of the cover.

The writer gratefully acknowledges the use of photographs from the following sources: Netherlands Music Institute, the Hague, where I always found a cheerful helper in Katja Brooymans. 'Hartelijk dank, Katja!' The Municipal Museum of the Hague; The Municipal Archives of Amsterdam; N.V. Het Concertgebouw Orkest, Amsterdam; The Lebrecht Music Collection, London.

From the start in 1999 my closest partner in this venture has, of course, been Rosamund Bartlett, mentioned earlier. What started as logistical support for someone else's hobby soon became a labour of love. Rosamund leads a busy academic life, including a good deal of travel, but she always found time for me and she put much of herself in the book. In the process she became a close personal friend of my wife and myself, a friendship we still treasure.

Finally, before going to press, I sent the manuscript to my daughter Sandra and her husband Tom, an accomplished scriptwriter. Their suggestions were helpful in improving readability, and I am very grateful to them.

The single most important relationship for a writer is with his designer and publisher. I have been fortunate in receiving constant support and constructive suggestions from Simon Stern and Morris Kahn. I hope they are pleased with the result of the collaboration.

I can vouch for the authenticity of the autographs and photographs. All I can say about the stories is that they are my own personal experiences. Whether the combination finds favour is for my readers to judge.

R.P.B.
Sotogrande, Spain summer 1999
Flims, Switzerland, winter 2002

Theo Olof

Foreword by Theo Olof

Back in the 1930s, not daily, but still very often, two young boys would stand at the Artists' Entrance of the Amsterdam Concertgebouw. Patiently and somewhat nervously they would wait for some famous artist to appear so they could beg him or her for their autograph. Usually they succeeded. And now, more than sixty years later, both having grown from being boys to jolly old fellows, and still great friends, the one who was the most assiduous autograph collector has asked the other, to wit myself, to write a short Foreword for this book containing his collection of autographs, together with appropriate and interesting explications. This friend, Robert Brouwer, became a successful businessman, but never lost his love for music and became a patron of the arts, while I, during my quite successful musical career as a concert violinist, had to give time and again my own autograph to musical fans, but remained quite jealous of Robert's collection of the world famous.

And now Robert, dear old boy, in this way at last I count myself lucky and proud, thanks to your request, to be permitted at last to join my autograph to your much envied collection.

Here you are, Robert, and here's to you! Cheerio!

Amsterdam 2002

Introduction

I was born and bred in Amsterdam, less than fifteen minutes by bicycle (everyone cycled) from the 'temple of music', the Concertgebouw. Amsterdam was in the thirties the musical capital of Europe, due to its outstanding orchestra and conductor Willem Mengelberg and to the near destruction by the Nazis of Berlin and Vienna as cultural centres. It may be argued that London was equally important, but it had spread its talents thinly over three orchestras (as it does today), whereas Amsterdam (a little chauvinism may be forgiven!) had its unique, superior orchestra, which, in addition to Mengelberg, attracted top class conductors like Bruno Walter, Pierre Monteux, Otto Klemperer, Georg Szèll and Erich Kleiber, and innumerable famous performing artists.

I had the advantage of having been brought up in an enlightened family, with a father who was interested in all the arts, and I was also lucky to have gone to a particularly enlightened school. It was founded by a man called Dr C. P. Gunning, who did not believe in rote learning, but in developing in his pupils at the earliest possible age an interest in all aspects of life, combined with a sense of individuality and responsibility. Hence there were a large number of extra-curricular activities on offer at the school: drama, music, photography, dancing, and of course sport. I was an active member of several clubs, but I was below average in sport, although not for lack of trying. In my lifetime I have played the obligatory hockey, afterwards graduating to tennis, cricket and later (too late!) to golf.

The only sport in which I achieved a degree of proficiency was riding. I did dressage and showjumping in regional tournaments. Music, however, soon became my great love, both as participant and listener. My parents had ordained that at the age of twelve I and my brother (who was ten) should learn the piano and the violin respectively, and so we did; I with enthusiasm, my brother more dutifully. Eventually my father had his due reward: a few years later my brother and I made a vinyl recording (still a complicated procedure in the thirties) of our playing, which was followed by spoken birthday wishes. Fortunately for listeners, this venture was never repeated.

I took my first steps in the Concertgebouw in 1934, at the age of thirteen, for a reason that was rather typical of my enterprising father. One Sunday morning a string on my brother's little violin snapped, and my father thought the best place to have it fixed was the Concertgebouw (which was rather like going to a fine cigar shop to buy a box of matches). The orchestra was giving a matinee concert that day, and in the intermission, any violinist could be accosted to fit a new string. I was allowed to accompany my father, probably just to carry the violin case. The violin gave us entry into the Concertgebouw, and we proceeded to the 'tuning room' of the orchestra. Opposite this room was a door leading to the platform, with a little glass spy window. The concert was still in progress and my father had to lift me up to see through the window. Then I saw for the first time a full orchestra in all its splendour, with an old gentleman in morning coat, standing in front of it, gesticulating. This was Carl Muck, the famous German conductor, who had worked with and conducted for Richard Wagner, along with the slightly older Hans Richter. He was by then seventy-five years old. Before the First World War, Carl Muck had conducted in America numerous times,

The author

but when he went back afterwards, he was booed as he was German. This was also the fate that awaited the famous German pianist Walter Gieseking after the Second World War. Neither ever went back. Muck had already lived through the 1870 war and the First World War, and died in 1940, just after the outbreak of the Second World War. Suffice it to say that a kindly violinist fixed the string of my brother's quarter-size violin.

Soon afterwards I conceived the idea that if I could not go and actually hear famous musicians in concert (since I was really too young still at that time), asking for their autographs was another matter and within my grasp. I spent my pocket money on purchasing an autograph book with pastel-coloured pages. Most concerts started at a quarter past eight in the evening and I was allowed to cycle to the Concertgebouw before half-past seven, but had to come back immediately after my mission was completed (which I did, in all kinds of weather). The following stories are really anecdotes, for the most part based on my collection of autographs, which were all assembled by me in person, and initially while I was still a little person (fourteen years of age). I was repeatedly offered autographs collected by others, such as those of Puccini, Toscanini (who never conducted in Amsterdam due to a longstanding feud with Mengelberg; both had been conductors for many years at the New York Philharmonic and Mengelberg often made derogatory remarks about Toscanini), Richard Strauss (who did come to Amsterdam but whom I missed) and Furtwängler, but I always refused them. I was even offered money for my collection, but that I also refused. Collecting autographs led – how, I will explain later- to turning pages for pianists in concert, and the two activities formed, at least for me, a rich source of anecdotal material. I hope some of it will interest readers too.

Robert Bremer

Flims, Switzerland, Winter 2002

1

From Autograph Hunter to Page Turner
Musicians at the Concertgebouw 1934-40

At the age of about fourteen, I met a violin prodigy two years younger than myself, who came with his mother as a refugee from Germany. His name was Theo Olof Schmuckler. Soon after his arrival, he was put in the care of Professor Oscar Back, also a refugee from Germany, and a world-renowned pedagogue. A godmother was also found for him in the person of Mrs Boissevain, a wonderful and caring lady who took Olof to her heart until the war (she lost her husband and a son in Resistance work). Mrs Boissevain felt that Olof had, as soon as possible, to assimilate in Holland and learn the language. Since I was about his age, loved music and lived nearby, I was asked to become his friend and playmate. I was happy to oblige and thereafter played a lot with him, so much so that one day, when he had to give a concert, we had so much fun that he dissolved in laughter and could not stop. He barely made it to the concert hall with a straight face and after that I was forbidden to play with him on a concert day. Olof was indeed very gifted and soon had an opportunity to play the Paganini D Major Concerto with Bruno Walter and the Concertgebouw Orchestra. Walter rarely bothered about prodigies, as he believed they had plenty of time to prove that their gifts were lasting. The story goes that before the concert he said: "You can play with me, but not as Theo Olof Schmuckler. I was born Bruno Walter Schlesinger and became Bruno Walter. From now on you will be Theo Olof." It is a nice story, but its veracity is somewhat in doubt. In fact it recently transpired that Bruno Walter was just Bruno Schlesinger. He took the Walter from the character of Walther in *Die Meistersinger*.

And so Theo remained Theo Olof for the rest of his life. I and other friends close to him had always called him Olof (or Olo), and years later I occasionally slipped back into that habit. People always wondered why I, as one of his oldest friends, still called him Olof! Theo, as is well known, had the career his talents promised; his concerts started soon after his arrival in Holland and continued up to the war, which he survived in hiding in Belgium, and then resumed after the war. He was a prizewinner at the Queen Elizabeth Concours in Brussels, and had a prospering solo career. Later he was offered the security of the first concertmastership of the (now Royal) Concertgebouw Orchestra in conjunction with his old friend Herman Krebbers, also a pupil of Oscar Back, in order for both of them to alternate and continue their solo careers. Olof and I always kept in touch. I had the pleasure of bringing him to Hong Kong where I lived in the seventies, to play the Tchaikovsky concerto with the Hong Kong Philharmonic Orchestra. Theo also managed to preserve his playful talents. For years he wrote a light-hearted column in a major Dutch newspaper, once directed a musical show and generally showed interest in all aspects of life. He always regretted that in his younger years he could not play football on the street or go ice-skating. On the serious side, he was the founder of the National Music Instrument Fund, which acquires string instruments for deserving young musicians. Recently, he celebrated his 75th birthday and is still in great demand as a jury member at violin competitions.

The point I wish to make is that while musicians of great talent are extraordinary people and lead extraordinary lives, they have at the same time ordinary needs and wishes. This is stating the obvious, but for friends to put this into practice is not always easy. It is with friends that talented musicians often want to do ordinary things, such as go cycling, go to the movies or travel, and friends should oblige and treat them as ordinary people. At the same time they should never forget that they are dealing with highly sensitive individuals who may abruptly act or react in an unexpected way. To deal with them in that vein is what friends are for. As it happens, Theo Olof offstage has always been the most normal and accessible of friends, but he is an exception.

My extra-curricular activities have always brought me into contact with musical celebrities, and I enjoyed this so much that after a while I actively sought their company, and continued to do so throughout my life. It sometimes demanded a subtle middle way between professional and social intercourse, but where this was achieved I found the relationship most rewarding and not at all one-sided. And now to the subject which was the reason why you bought, borrowed or picked up this book: my autograph collection and the little stories behind it. I will only select musicians who still have fame today, large or small, or who in other ways were out of the ordinary.

The first signature I wish to show is that of **Willem Mengelberg** (1871-1951), with the principal theme of Richard Strauss' *Also sprach Zarathustra*. And I hope you will bear with me when I devote a little more attention to him. The reasons are that for fifty years Mengelberg was the heart of Holland's musical life, a much wanted guest conductor overseas (he was music director of the New York Philharmonic from 1922 to 1930, when Toscanini took over), who conducted in practically all the European capitals. He was, it was said, the best-known person in Holland after Queen Wilhemina, and last

Willem Mengelberg with Alma Mahler, widow of Gustav Mahler, 4th April 1912. His autograph, (below) includes the principal theme of Also sprach Zarathustra. The inscription reads 'In memory of the concert, 1. XII Amsterdam.'

but not least, as far as I was concerned, he was responsible for shaping much of my musical education. He was born in 1871 and at the age of twenty-seven took over the directorship of the Concertgebouw Orchestra. This was a year after a visit by Brahms, who drily commented that the Dutch were nice people but poor musicians. He was right. The orchestra was undisciplined, had an indifferent conductor who nevertheless went on to a degree of fame in England, and an audience which drank coffee and also talked and walked around during concerts. What is practically forgotten is that Mengelberg was also an excellent pianist. Before taking over the music directorship, he made his debut with a Liszt Piano Concerto. In a few years he whipped the orchestra into a shape on which Mahler in the early 1900s commented most favourably. Mahler was at that time conductor of the Vienna State Opera.

Mengelberg is today often summarily dismissed as a romantic conductor (in the pejorative sense), as compared, for example, with the purist Toscanini. It should be remembered that Mengelberg's formative years fell squarely in the 19th century, when conductors were expected – also by composers – to give a personal interpretation of a work. Mengelberg did that and had the musical personality to make a lasting impression on his audience. By contrast it is said that Toscanini let the composer and the score speak for themselves without any discretionary freedom on the part of the conductor. This is not true: Toscanini retouched the orchestration of the storm movement in Beethoven's Sixth Symphony, for example, and is known to have added timpani in other works when he deemed it effective. A striking example is his recording of Schuman's Second Symphony, where you hear the changes he made in the trumpet part in the coda of the first movement, as well as a trumpet flourish he added to the last movement. Mengelberg took great liberties with dynamics and tempi and doubled winds in major symphonic works, but never added or deleted a note.

An exception may have been a Mahler orchestration. In matters of orchestration Mahler told a few close friends like Bruno Walter or Willem Mengelberg: 'You know what I want to achieve. If you can think of a better way of achieving it, please feel free.' Toscanini was even older than Mengelberg and developed his authentic style early on in life and in that sense was more than a generation ahead of his time and unique among contemporaries. However, his style did not always find approval. Furtwängler called him a metronome. The general impression was indeed that his tempi were fast and this was true in, for instance, Beethoven. In Wagner they were exceptionally slow. His *Parsifal* at Bayreuth was the slowest in the history of that house, one hour slower than the fastest under Richard Strauss. Mengelberg did play Bach, but mainly the *St Matthew Passion*, in an abbreviated and romanticised form, a cantata or two and a few orchestral works. He played little Mozart or Haydn but his great love was Beethoven, which he played in a heroic fashion. He played all major 19th-century composers up to Tchaikovsky, and then came his second great love, Mahler, who was his ten-years older contemporary. They

Mengelberg conducting.

became close friends and Mahler was quoted as saying that Mengelberg conducted his works better than he did himself. Mahler was unquestionably one of the greatest conductors of his time, in fact more admired as conductor than as composer. He visited Amsterdam frequently. One première was unusual in that Mahler conducted his 4th Symphony first, to be repeated after the intermission by Mengelberg, a practice still to be commended today. The other Mahler champion was of course Bruno Walter, an equally close friend. When we today speak of Mengelberg's extravaganzas it may be well to remember that in 1907, after he conducted Tchaikovsky's 6th Symphony, the composer's younger brother mounted the podium, embraced Mengelberg and said "Ah Monsieur Mengelberg, enfin les tempi de mon frère!"

The first great Mahler festival was held in 1920 by Mengelberg in Amsterdam with Alma Mahler, the composer's widow, present throughout. In the thirties, no audience knew Mahler better than Amsterdam. I remember an overwhelming performance of Mahler's 8th Symphony in 1938, the 'Symphony of a Thousand', which in this case numbered perhaps four hundred. A few days later our school class was asked to write an essay on a subject of our own choice. I chose this performance and won first prize (I promise no more self-congratulatory remarks). It is worth noting that Mengelberg was born of German parents in Utrecht where his father had found work sculpting church effigies. Mengelberg spoke German at home and Dutch at school and remained bilingual all his life. His annotations in scores were often in German. As soon as he finished school, he went to Cologne in Germany to start his musical education under Franz Wuellner. His first post was as choir conductor in Switzerland.

The chauvinistic streak in the Dutch adoration of Mengelberg totally ignored the fact that from his young days he had described himself as a 'Deutsch-Niederländer' (he always used the expression in German), and was proud to wear that label. Considering his birth and upbringing, anything else would have been surprising. All professional conductors need to have a certain autocratic bias, and Mengelberg perhaps possessed this quality more than others. Mengelberg did not always bully. At one rehearsal, where he could not get the orchestra to stop talking, he said "Anyone who talks in rehearsal pays twenty five cents, proceeds going to charity," whereupon a bright young thing among the violins got up and said "Mr Mengelberg, I would like to pay right now two guilders-worth of 'chat money'." Actually, in his early years, before World War I, Mengelberg himself was the target of sometimes cruel jokes from the orchestra and several times asked for a representative of the Board to be present at rehearsals as a kind of 'policeman'.

Reverting for a minute to Mengelberg's musical profile, apart from Mahler, he also championed composers like Richard Strauss, who dedicated *Ein Heldenleben* to him. The motif in my autograph book is the main theme of *Also sprach Zarathustra*, which he had just performed in concert. Another composer who found a regular contemporary interpreter in Mengelberg was Stravinsky. More about him when his autograph appears. It is worth mentioning that Mengelberg (who, as I have said, was totally German-educated and in his own words considered Germany his second 'Heimat') once issued an invitation to Hindemith, whose music and person were banned from Germany in 1937 by Goebbels as 'Entartete Kunst' (degenerate art). Mengelberg invited Hindemith to conduct his *Mathis der Mahler* symphony and a few days later the composer played the viola solo in *Der Schwanendreher* with Mengelberg conducting. A nearly forgotten episode was Mengelberg's invitation to Schoenberg to visit Amsterdam. Between October 1920 and April 1921 Schoenberg taught courses in composition and musical analysis, and conducted the Concertgebouw Orchestra in several concerts of his own works. When a composer conducted his own work, Mengelberg sometimes had the habit of joining the orchestra, for example, as a tympanist. Another example of Mengelberg's support of contemporary music is in the Netherlands Music Festival which he organised in 1935 on the occasion of his jubilee marking the fortieth anniversary of his appointment as conductor of the Concertgebouw Orchestra. What is rarely remembered is that he gave a similar Festival as early as 1902.

It is true that in his later years he tended to concentrate on the classic and romantic repertoire. I had the good fortune of being able to hear Mengelberg at numerous concerts – not the subscription concerts which were too expensive and to which my father went – but the so-called 'popular concerts' which cost Fls 0,64, including 11 cents 'amusement tax', and were given almost weekly. I also heard four years running from 1936 his annual Beethoven cycle. Mengelberg was in those years the most decorated Dutchman, and on his sixtieth birthday he received a car as a gift from his grateful public. "The sound of the engine is music in my ears" he said.

A few words about the superior qualities of Mengelberg's Concertgebouw Orchestra which are apparent to this day. First of all he had no problem recruiting the best string players locally. The orchestra had international fame and was relatively well-endowed. The chairman for many years was Dr. H. Heineken, of Heineken beer fame, who was a good pianist himself and played occasionally with the orchestra, for example, at pension fund benefits. His son, also chairman of Heineken, who recently passed away, and was known for his being kidnapped for ransom some years ago, was also a maecenas, but more for the popular arts (a pity for the Concertgebouw). From his wind players Mengelberg demanded "solo tone" (sound that stood out in the orchesra), and for this he often went to Germany to recruit players. When I heard the orchestra, the principal flautist, Hubert Barwahser, the principal clarinettist, Rudolf Gall and the principal horn player, Rudolf Szell, were all German. The timpanist, Vater, was also German, but soon replaced by a Dutchman.

There are many stories about Mengelberg's erratic and autocratic behaviour during rehearsal. A recent Dutch biography, researched in great detail, discussed at length his conduct on and off-stage in order to expose the faults in which a great man can be small, only to discover that these are the exact same faults in which a small man is small. The idea of a partnership between conductor and orchestra, undisputed today, was unheard of and unpractised in the first half of the twentieth century, and even today there are exceptions. Mengelberg could also be rude, but which conductor is not occasionally? Solti in London was called by an unkind press 'the screaming skull'. I once attended a rehearsal of Beethoven's 9th symphony, and after the choir's entry, Mengelberg remarked "What you are singing is the German word for scabies, *Räude*, which indeed sounds almost identical to *Freude*."

Mengelberg was also known to spend a great deal of rehearsal time talking, sometimes for most of the rehearsal. I recall a music critic with excellent credentials asking him one day the reason for this, and Mengelberg replied laconically "If you have built up a repertoire meticulously over twenty five years with the same orchestra there is no need to rehash every detail at every rehearsal. It can in fact be self-defeating." This was confirmed to me by my good friend, the first oboe, **Haakon Stotijn** (1915-1963), probably the single most valuable player in the orchestra, to whom Mengelberg once said during rehearsal of the second movement of Brahms' First Symphony: "If you play this so beautifully tonight, I may start crying." Stotijn confirmed that rehearsals were not always a big

deal, but he added "in performance the spark never failed." As an antidote to boring rehearsals, orchestra members did what orchestra members do all over the world – they played chess, did crosswords, or, as one Frenchman did, read *Le Monde*. "Where else can I read it?" he used to say. They also occasionally showed their annoyance when new works were rehearsed. I remember the second flautist telling me one day that for a whole movement he played two tones too low, unnoticed by Mengelberg. Incidentally, speaking about flutes, a monster fund-raising concert was once held in the Amsterdam Olympic stadium built for the Olympic games in 1927, by the combined The Hague and Amsterdam orchestras under Mengelberg. Next morning, a cartoon by Holland's foremost caricaturist, Jo Spier, showed a vast stadium with a tiny Mengelberg peering over the edge and the passing local train to Amstelveen whistling in the background and Mengelberg holding up a finger saying "I hear a flute too many."

Mengelberg's behaviour during the war is too well-known to require description here. He had no doubt German sympathies, but not in the political sense. He certainly paid heavily for his behaviour or misbehaviour by being barred for life 'in absentia' in 1945 by a Special Commission from conducting in Holland. He was also deprived of all royal decorations awarded to him during the past 50 years.

In 1947 an appeal before a Central Council of Honour was heard, supported by members of the orchestra, including Jewish members, and Eduard van Beinum, Mengelberg's successor as Principal Conductor of the orchestra. This revue resulted in the reduction of the life sentence to seven years. Mengelberg was unable to attend the proceedings as his passport had been taken away. When he learned of the sentence he wrote a brief statement to the effect that for fifty years he had faithfully served Holland, Amsterdam and the Concergetbouw Orchestra. All this came too late: he died two months before the expiry of his sentence in 1951 at the age of eighty in his 'Chasa Mengelberg' in Switzerland.

As counterpoint to Mengelberg's attitude during the war let me mention a few facts which bear out his conviction that he had only lived for his music, a statement other musicians made less convincingly. During the first year of the German occupation, and aginst explicit orders from Goebbels and Seyss Inquart, the Austrian Nazi ruler of Holland, Mengelberg programmed and played a concert of works by Mendelsohn and

Willem Mengelberg in old age in exile in the chapel of his Swiss chalet.

Mahler (his first symphony), - both Jewish composers - something no-one had ever dared to do in Germany, not even Furtwängler.

He also succeeded in saving several Jewish members of the orchestra from concentration camp and certain death (a.o. Hubert Bahrwasser, the principal flautist). This became known during the 1990s in a letter from Israel.

During his exile in Switzerland Mengelberg received numerous invitations to conduct in Europe, America and even in Russia, to which he invariably replied: "As soon as I am able to conduct my own orchestra first."

As a personal footnote, I would like to mention that this Swiss chalet where he died was built by him in 1911, on a spot he discovered while on a walking tour of the area. It was on a mountain-side in one of the most inaccessible areas of Switzerland. Mengelberg bought the elevated site (friends always said that Mengelberg loved mountains, but "from a point of view of equality") and built a large chalet where he spent time every summer. He was looked after until his death by a young violinist in the orchestra, Miss Elly Bysterus Heemskerk, who acted as his hostess and housekeeper (more about her later). Tilly Mengelberg, Mengelberg's wife, also liked Switzerland, but not beyond Zürich or Luzern. In the seventies, Miss Heemskerk - or Aunt Elly as she was called - invited me to spend a few days at Chasa Mengelberg in Zuort in the Engadin, which had been turned into a recuperation centre for ailing orchestra members.

Aunt Elly still ran the chalet, with some help, every summer, although she was by then already in her eighties. I accepted the invitation, which involved a bus ride, followed by half an hour in a jeep through uncharted territory. I found the chalet full of perfectly healthy orchestra members and their families, who obviously were enjoying a free Swiss holiday. Mengelberg, who was Catholic, had built adjacent to the chalet a charming wooden chapel with a carillon, which he played daily at sunset. Aunt Elly continued this habit, which I found quite moving. I spent much of my time going over Mengelberg's guest books, now presumably in his archives in The Hague, which showed every conceivable celebrity visiting between 1911 and 1940 (Prince Hendrik of the Netherlands, Richard Strauss, Stravinsky, Fritz Kreisler, Pierre Monteux), all with personalized entries. It was a real treasure trove. Mengelberg wrote the connecting commentary, mostly in German, referring to himself as 'Onkel-Hausfrau' (Uncle-housewife).

Eduard van Beinum (1900-1959), whose signature comes next, was Principal Conductor of the Concertgebouw Orchestra from 1938, jointly with Willem Mengelberg, and after 1945 sole Principal Conductor until his death in 1959. He was a complete contrast to Mengelberg If the latter was an authoritarian, van Beinum was a 'co-operative' conductor. As a former member of the orchestra who had played under both conductors put it: "You played under Mengelberg, but you played with van Beinum." This had its drawbacks. Van Beinum never lost patience with the orchestra (although he admitted losing patience with himself) and as a result his rehearsal discipline was poor. There were

Eduard van Beinum, Mengelberg's successor and below, his autograph.

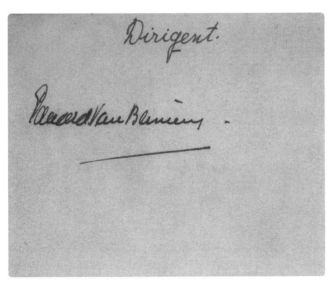

times when the orchestra sent a delegation to him asking to pull the reins a little tighter. Nevertheless he set the tone for the future (doing away with Mengelberg's extravagances along the way and going back to the score), and will always be remembered as one of the great conductors of the century. Van Beinum also became Principal Conductor of the London Philharmonic Orchestra and later the Los Angeles Philharmonic Orchestra, where he was equally loved. A leading player of the Los Angeles Philharmonic once said to van Beinum: "You have opened up the heart of this orchestra after years in the deep freeze." In 1950 a serious heart condition was diagnosed and at that time little could be done for him. Van Beinum never slowed down. A particularly strenuous period came when the Concertgebouw undertook its first American tour in 1954, and van Beinum conducted thirty concerts in the space of a few weeks, and had in addition to cope with the exertions of travel and social engagements. He never complained. Eduard van Beinum died as he would have wished, in full harness, as it were, having collapsed during a rehearsal on 11 April 1959. A similar fate was encountered by his fellow conductors Dmitri Mitropoulos in 1960 while rehearsing Mahler's Symphony No. 3, Joseph Keilberth, Music Director of the Bavarian State Opera, who died following a performance of *Tristan und Isolde* in 1968, and Giuseppe Sinopoli who died during a performance of *Aida* at the Deutsche Oper in Berlin in 2001.

The violinist **Bronislaw Huberman** (1882-1947), who was born in Poland, received advice from Joachim, for whom Brahms wrote his Violin Concerto (a concerto Joachim called not "for the violin" but "against the violin"). Joachim was so proud of his pupil that he let the young boy play it for Brahms a year before his death. A few years later, I turned the pages for his partner, Ignaz Friedman and so had the opportunity to watch this kind man from close quarters. Huberman was the founder of the Palestine Orchestra, as it was called then. He was very politically engaged, and loved having political discussions before and after concerts. In Amsterdam he sometimes played string quartets with his Dutch friends, followed by a political discourse. He was one of the plainest people I have ever seen. He was a small man with a yellow complexion and a large squint, and when he stood in front of the piano during his Concertgebouw recital, one eye seemed be looking at me all the time, as I turned the pages for his accompanist. When he played, however, his face became transfigured with a transcendental expression, like that of Casals. It is no more than fair to point out that he had survived a plane crash a few years earlier and had recovered through sheer willpower, but with the scars still visible. Isaac Stern told me once that he considered Huberman one of the greatest violinists of the twentieth century. Huberman was one of the first violinists to play concertos by the three "Bs" (Bach, Beethoven and Brahms) in one concert.

Wilhelm Backhaus (1884-1969), was probably the most famous German pianist of his time, especially in Beethoven and Brahms, a reputation which continues to this day. His is the first autograph to which there is a personal anecdote attached. On the day of

Opposite page: the violinist Bronislaw Huberman, founder of the Palestine Orchestra (left) and Wilhelm Backhaus, probably the most famous German pianist of his time (right).

Violist.

Bronislaw Hubermann
10.I.1936.

Dem ausgezeichneten Kofferträger
mit besten Grüssen
Wilhelm Backhaus

4. Februar 1936

Pianist.

The soprano, Jo
Vincent, who had a
down-to-earth sense of
humour, in a recital
accompanied by
Mengelberg.

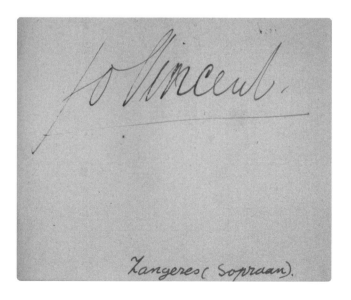

Turning the Pages

his concert, I waited for him at the artists' entrance of the Concertgebouw, and he arrived in a taxi followed by a large suitcase. He came out and when I greeted him he said, "I will give you my signature, but first how do we get this suitcase up to the soloist's room?" I tried to lift it and just about managed it, but it weighed a ton, and the soloist's room was four staircases up, with no lift. There was no one else around to help (the doorman could not leave his post), so I had to try. I was fourteen years old and tall for my age, but obviously did not have the necessary muscles. I do not know how I managed it, but I got the suitcase into the soloist's room. I found Backhaus sitting alone in the room and he at once asked me, "Do you know why this suitcase is so heavy? It is full of wrong notes." Then he signed my book, as you can see, "Dem ausgezeichneten Koffer-träger, mit besten Grüssen" – 'to the excellent porter with my best greetings.' His preferred composer was Brahms and this preference may go back to the time when Backhaus was ten years old and saw Brahms conduct his own two piano concertos with Eugène D'Albert as soloist.

Jo Vincent (1898-1989) is still today little known outside Holland, but in her time she was an outstanding soprano. Toscanini invited her once for a *Missa Solemnis* in Vienna. She was mainly a Lieder and Oratorio singer, but I remember hearing her once as the Countess in *Le Nozze di Figaro*, sung, as was the custom before the war, in German. She had a pure and crystal-clear soprano, and her voice may have come from heaven, but her feet were firmly on the ground. She loved off-colour jokes, and I remember one time travelling with her and another singer in a car to Arnhem where they were to sing the *St. Matthew Passion* under the conductorship of my piano teacher's father and she started on her repertoire. The other lady said "No, Jo, not in front of the boy," whereupon Jo Vincent said "Either he is too young to understand or old enough and then it doesn't matter." An hour later she was singing in the church like an angel.

Erich Kleiber (1890-1956) was the first of the great German conductors to leave Germany in 1934, and he did so with a flourish. He was always supporting modern music, and performed *Symphonic Pieces* from the opera *Lulu* by Alban Berg, against the express orders of Goebbels, on the 30th November 1934. Within weeks Kleiber left Germany. He didn't wait for a reaction from Goebbels.

He went to Argentina, where they were happy to make him music director of the famous Teatro Colon. His wife was American and it was in Buenos Aires that his son was born. They named him Carlos. Carlos has become now every bit as good a conductor as his father, but more reclusive. After the war Erich Kleiber returned to Europe for guest performances, and it was here that he died, in the Grand Hotel Dolder in Zürich. Many years later I was having a drink with friends at this hotel, and I told them that Kleiber died here. Then quietly and respectfully a waiter came up to me and said "Excuse me sir, but you might be interested to know that it was I who discovered Mr Kleiber in his bathroom. He died of a heart attack."

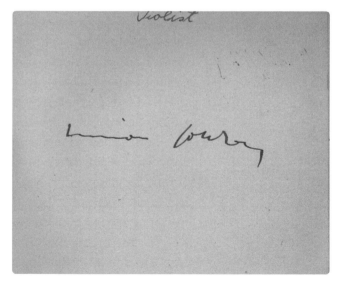

Opposite page: left, Erich Kleiber, who conducted Hindemith's Mathis der Mahler against the orders of Goebbels and right, the violinist Szymon Golberg. It was his partner, Lili Kraus (this page) who started my career as a page turner when she asked me if I could read music too.

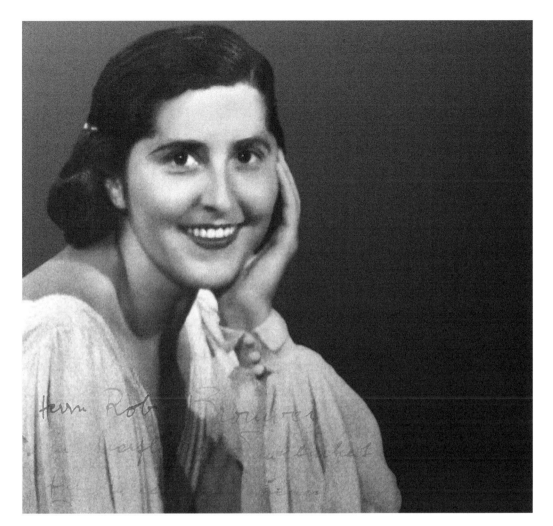

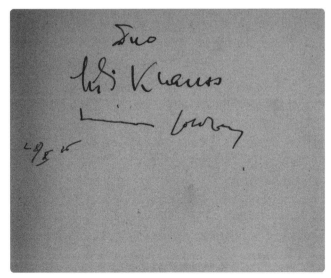

We now come, literally, to a turning point in my life as an autograph hunter. It was the evening of my 15th birthday, 18 October 1936 and I was waiting at the artists' entrance of the Concertgebouw for a beautiful young lady, the pianist **Lili Kraus** (1905-1986). She arrived in a taxi, wearing a fur coat, and was followed by a young man, her age, carrying a violin case. This was **Szymon Goldberg** (1909-1995). She was also accompanied by a much older, bald gentleman, dressed in a dark suit and dark hat whom I took to be her manager. It turned out he was her husband, a philosophy professor named Otto Mandl. He was exquisitely courteous to everyone, but distant, also to his wife, and practically invisible before and after the concerts, also during intermission. When I asked Lili Kraus for her autograph, she asked me in German whether I could read music too? I had no idea why she asked that question, but I said yes. She then said "In that case, you will turn the pages for me tonight" and she took me up to the artist's room. I still didn't quite understand what she meant, but she soon explained it to me, and showed me her scores. "But first," she said, "I must call your parents and tell them what you are doing tonight, and that you are safe with me." So she did, and my father fortunately agreed. She then introduced me to her partner, the violinist Szymon Goldberg, who sometimes wrote his name the Western way, Simon, and sometimes Szymon, as he was born Polish. And on we went. I had no problems with the music, as I played the piano myself. It was a Mozart and Beethoven sonata programme, and she had shown me, and also marked clearly in the score, the repeats. At that age you have no nerves, no stage fright, and Lili seemed pleased with me. Her husband afterwards also thanked me.

Lili Kraus had an expressive and natural beauty, as her photo bears out. She wore no make-up except for lipstick, and perhaps a dab of powder, and she had dark brown eyes, the colour of her hair, which was neatly parted on the side and fell to her shoulders. She had a sparkling nature, with sudden moments of reflectiveness you always knew would be there. Maybe the best way to describe her was that she had the spirit of Mozart - overflowing with freedom and gaiety but with a depth of feeling - a composer of whose music she was a supreme interpreter. She rarely walked, always danced, up the stairs, up the platform, but walked back slowly, as if reluctant to leave it. That night she wore a long shining black taffeta dress, beautifully cut, with a wide skirt, which swirled around her legs and covered at least three feet of floor when she sat down. She wore no jewellery, except a wedding ring, which she wore on her left hand. Over the next four years I became a regular fixture at her concerts. She was born in Budapest in 1905 and received her musical training at the Budapest Academy of Music (piano with Bartók, composition with Kodály), graduating in 1922. At this stage she was known as a Chopin pianist. After her debut in Holland, she continued her studies with Artur Schnabel in Berlin. Her partnership with Goldberg began in 1934 and was to last nine years.

She developed, or rather we developed, two rituals during her playing. First she took off her wedding ring and put it on the piano next to the keyboard. To me it had an almost symbolic meaning that she put her marriage on hold while she was married to her music. Sometimes she forgot the ring after the concert and I brought it to her. I once asked her whether she shouldn't give it to me to keep during the concert and she quietly shook her head. The other ritual was that she would sometimes be overcome by the emotion of the music, and tears would actually run down her cheek. Before the concert she would give me her handkerchief, and after a movement, if she dropped her left hand beside the chair, I had to put the handkerchief into her hand. Cycling home that night, I realised that for the first time in my life I had fallen in love. Lili Kraus returned my affection by asking me to babysit for her children, Ruth and Michael, who were about six and four years old, and sometimes invited me to her birthday party (she was living in Amsterdam at that time), introducing me as "almost a member of the family."

She escaped Holland in time to avoid the war, but she was on tour, in the Dutch East Indies, now Indonesia, in December 1941, when the Japanese overran that country. She was interned, and spent the remaining years until August 1945 in a camp. People who met her after the liberation told me that she seemed to have lost her perpetual youth and vivacity after the war years, but it may simply have been a matter of growing older. I met Lili Kraus again and for the last time thirty years later in Hong Kong, where I then lived. She was on a private visit and she looked as beautiful as ever. She was then over 60, a little fragile, like a Meissen porcelain doll, with little crackly lines around her eyes and mouth. I still loved the Lili Kraus of thirty years before and I think she knew it. At that time she lived in London where she continued her concert and recording career, to great public and critical acclaim, although she perhaps did not altogether live up to the admittedly very high expectations she created before the war. She was the first to record all Mozart piano sonatas, even before Nadia Reisenberg did. Her partnership with Szymon Goldberg had come to an end. Eventually she moved to America where she died, in 1986. It is hard to realise that my last meeting with Lili Kraus is now also some thirty years back.

In the same breath, I should mention Szymon Goldberg, her partner. Goldberg was about the same age as Lili Kraus, a very quiet, almost self-effacing man, always neatly groomed. He was born in 1909 in Poland and went to Berlin to study with Carl Flesch, becoming one of his favourite pupils. At the age of twelve, he made his debut with the D major Paganini Concerto (as did, interestingly, Theo Olof), and on Flesch's advice became Concertmaster of the Dresden Philharmonic, moving in 1930 to the Berlin Philharmonic under Furtwängler as the youngest Concertmaster ever in Berlin. It was a short-lived experience, with a dramatic ending. Due to the racial laws of Germany, he had to leave in 1934, although Furtwängler made a personal representation, even in writing, on his behalf to his Nazi friends. Goldberg did not wait for the outcome of these representations and left Germany. This episode actually got a mention in Ronald Harwood's recent play on Furtwängler, *Taking Sides*.

In Amsterdam, Szymon Goldberg met his old friend Paul Godwin, who had made a great deal of money in Germany leading a famous dance band. He had to go underground before escaping to Holland. After settling in Amsterdam he re-formed what he called his "amusement orchestra" which played nightly in a well-known restaurant in Amsterdam. Godwin was born Pinchas Goldfain in 1902 and studied violin under a famous teacher, Jenö Hubay in Budapest, in whose house he lived, and then with Willy Hess. In 1934 he emigrated to Holland. He had to leave his considerable fortune behind. During the war he went underground and had to work repairing airfields. After the war, from 1952 to 1970, he played viola in the greatest of Dutch string quartets, the Netherlands Quartet, with Nap de Klijn, Jaap Schröder and Carel van Leeuwen Boomkamp.

Goldberg was captured by the Japanese in Java in 1942. It is fortunate that because of her ill-health the Japanese left behind one lady who was also living in the house where Goldberg was taken prisoner. This lady apparently saved Goldberg's Stradivarius by throwing it over a fence into the garden of an amateur violinist, who in turn passed it on to a Swiss family and they, as citizens of a neutral country, were able to keep it and return it to Goldberg after the war! Goldberg survived his internment in a camp in Java, but the partnership Kraus-Goldberg was never revived after the war. He had a long and successful solo career, and outlived Lili Kraus by many years.

For several years after the war Goldberg was conductor of the Netherlands Chamber Orchestra, before Antonio Ros Marba (from Madrid) and David Zinman (from Baltimore and now Zürich).

Soon after my debut as page-turner, I was approached by the foremost music impresario in Amsterdam, a man called De Koos - an eminently Dutch name, but I soon found out that De Koos was Hungarian. De Koos in fact was a Hungarian émigré who made a successful business in the 1920s as an impresario. He was a physically imposing man, and had a reputation of not being easy to live with. He tapped me on the shoulder and said "It seems you feel rather at ease on the platform, and I would like to make you a proposition. Every time you turn the pages at one of my concerts, I will give you two guilders fifty. Two and half guilders at that time was more than twice my weekly pocket money, and therefore a very tempting offer. But the cheeky young man I was, I said, "No sir, may I make another proposal. I will turn the pages at your concerts for free, if on the nights when I don't have to turn pages, you will give me a free concert ticket." This was of course a much better deal for De Koos, since the ticket did not cost him any money, and it was a much better deal for me too, since in this way I was able to hear a large number of concerts for free.

Most of the following autographs were therefore collected 'after work', or after attending a free concert. Over the years I developed a rapport with many pianists who tended to return every season, not only because I was a good music reader but because I was tall for my age, had long arms, and could turn pages without getting up from my chair - which most turners did, at some inconvenience to the pianist - but leaning over the keyboard while remaining seated. It also meant that my head would come close to the pianist, who could give me last minute instructions, for example, that a written repeat would not be played. I was young and impressionable, which made it easy for the pianists to talk to me, and I had one rule, which was only to speak when spoken to. The artists could speak to me in four languages: German, French, English, and of course Dutch. With hindsight it is surprising how little English was spoken.

I was also adept at extra-curricular services, such as getting a drink when no waiter was around, or calling a taxi after a concert. The artists' room had no external telephone. I was in league with all the staff of the Concertgebouw, who could be relied upon to let me through wherever I wanted to go, into the kitchen, or even the staff quarters. No door was locked for me, and those who are familiar with concert halls or opera houses know that ninety percent of all doors are closed to the public. I would usually come early, say at seven thirty for a concert starting at a quarter past eight, in order to be briefed on the programme, repeats and edited parts, as well as transcriptions, which would be pasted over or extended, sometimes a foot outside the page of a score. This also gave the artist a chance to get used to my physical presence, which would always be very quiet. Artists are invariably tense before a concert and demand privacy.

I was also generally in charge of all sheet music, including the violinists' and the cellists' parts, and the scores of all possible encores, which would be chosen at the last minute. This made for a heavy and rather bulky load (since often just one sonata would be played out of an entire volume) which all had to be taken down at the start. Access to the platform was a bit complicated. I described earlier that for Wilhelm Backhaus I had to lug a heavy suitcase full of piano music from the entrance to the soloists' room. This room is situated at the level of the balcony, four floors of broad staircases up. A corridor ran the length of the balcony with entrances at intervals to the balcony seats. The soloist's room was also along this corridor some sixty feeet on the opposite side from the entrance leading to the platform. Next to this entrance was the Chairman's Box – not as one would expect in the middle of the balcony, 'facing the music'. Artists could descend to the platform either directly through a door from the corridor or through the Chairman's Box. The distance was the same either way and meant descending at least twenty-five awkward steps (too widely spaced for one step and too narrow to take two). Breaks in the programme had therefore to be carefully planned to avoid too many trips back. The Russian-born soprano Oda Slobodskaya, whom I will mention later, flatly refused to walk up and down the steps during the breaks. She had to be accommodated in a small space I conjured up in front of the organ manual, just a few steps up.

My practice with the scores was to leave music only needed after a break in the Chairman's Box, hoping it would not be tampered with. I would then retrieve it during the break. On a number of times during my long career an artist (usually a cellist or a lady singer) would decide on the spur of the moment not to go up the stairs during a break, preferring instead to stay put. I would have to fetch the music by myself in those cases. I remember one such occasion rather sprinting up the steps, which, on my return, provoked the comment by the pianist: "Don't run, walk."

These were thrilling nights, but any excitement felt was soon dampened by the home run on my bicycle. In the winter season in Amsterdam this mostly meant wind, darkness, rain or a combination of all three. Once I had a flat tyre on the way back. The realisation that I had to be up the next morning at seven to be at school at twenty past eight, once again on my bicycle, did not help at all. I am proud to say that in four years I never missed a class. On the other hand, a number of teachers who were keen concert goers and saw me on the platform developed a soft spot for me, and I took full advantage of it. I particularly remember my history teacher, a rather grumpy old man, who felt he had been passed over several times for university tenure, telling me one afternoon that he would like to attend that evening's concert but had discovered that it was sold out. At six o'clock I was able to telephone him and tell him that a complimentary ticket would be waiting for him at the box office. Mr de Koos told me that all the seats had been sold, but then said that he would give away a reserved fireman's seat. This was totally illegal of course.

Next is one of my prize autographs, the Spanish cellist **Pablo Casals** (1876-1973), signed beneath the opening bar of Bach's solo suite no 3. I turned the pages that night for his Austrian pianist **Otto Schulhoff**, whose signature appears on the next page, and who made a number of virtuoso adaptations of Strauss waltzes and polkas for the piano. He signed as Pau Casals, which is Catalan for Pablo. He was born in Catalonia and was a devoted republican. When Franco won in 1939, he left Spain, vowing never to return as long as he was in power. When I entered the artists' room I found Casals playing his

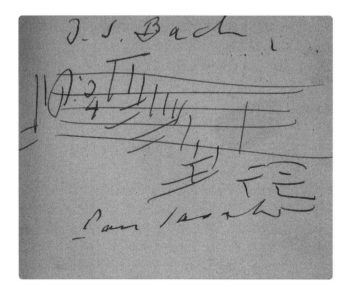
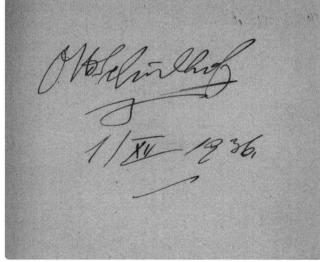

This page and opposite page left: Pablo Casals, a great cellist and political activist for a free Spain. Opposite page right: his accompanist Otto Schulhoff.

cello in shirt sleeves, his pipe in his mouth, and his steel-rimmed glasses half way down his nose. He beckoned to me and said "Young man, please walk up and down the room for me." I had received many strange requests before, but this was one of the most unusual. I walked up and down the room and then he said: "That is alright. The reason why I ask you is that I want you to turn the pages for me too, not only for the pianist, and that means walking round the piano, and we must make sure that your shoes don't creak. As regards my music, I don't read the score, I play by heart and my eyesight is so poor that I cannot read without glasses, which I don't wear in concert. But I don't want to upstage my pianist. We are partners. It doesn't matter when you turn the page – I suggest about here." I can only find one word to describe him while playing: transfigured. He was a short, bald man with a pug nose, altogether of unprepossessing appearance. When he played he used to turn his head sideways, in the direction of the piano, where I happened to be sitting, as if to say "hear how beautiful a cello can sound." He became one with the instrument. They swayed together while playing, and his face literally radiated. I was sitting not more than four metres away from him when he played one of the Bach cello suites. Casals was in a class by himself, in which he was later joined by Slava Rostropovich and Jacqueline du Pré. There were of course other famous cellists – Emmanuel Feuermann, Gregor Piatigorsky, Enrico Mainardi, Gaspar Cassadó and Pierre Fournier, for example, who were the Yo Yo Mas of their day.

We come to another famous name: **Arthur Rubinstein** (1887-1982), who was born in 1887, and lived into his nineties. In 1937 he was already famous as a pianist of all the great works, especially Chopin, but in his earlier years he made a reputation mainly as a promoter of modern music. On the night when I asked for his autograph, he played the first piano concerto of Tchaikovsky with the Concertgebouw Orchestra under Willem Mengelberg, and after the concert I went up to the artists' room to meet him. He was about to sign his autograph when he looked up and said "Young man, who won tonight's competition? Mr Mengelberg or I?" At which Mengelberg, who was standing nearby, interrupted and said "Of course, Arthur, you were ahead most of the time, but I think we finished together." A year later he opened the Golden Anniversary season of the Concertgebouw Orchestra and the story goes that after the concert he was taken by the Board to one of his favourite places, a night club in Amsterdam, called the Villa D'Este. The story goes on to say that he was unhappy with the pianist of the band and after a while moved on to the piano himself, sat down and played for an hour.

Personally I think this story is apocryphal, but *se non è vero...* There are still many Rubinstein stories doing the rounds, most of which he freely provided himself. He once said, when he was a young man "practice is a bad habit" and "when I look down at my hands, I see them doing amazing things, quite independently of myself." Perhaps these two remarks were the reflection of the extraordinary talent which had been given

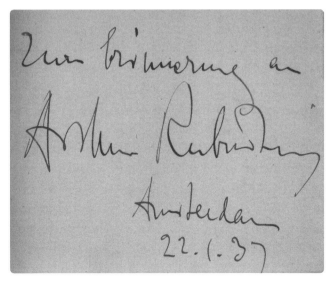

Arthur Rubinstein, *great pianist and great wit.*

to Rubinstein, and which was second only to Horowitz, who was twenty years younger. I turned pages only once for him, in the next year, when he gave a concert with the Guarneri String Quartet. When I presented myself in the artists' room, he welcomed me and said "I'm glad to see you, but I don't need your services. I play all my works by heart and my eyesight is anyway too weak to be able to see a mass of small notes printed on the page and I am too vain to wear glasses, but I don't want to upstage my partners, and therefore I ask you to turn the pages. If you miss one or two it doesn't matter" (shades of Casals). The ease with which Rubinstein performed so brilliantly gave him plenty of time for the pursuit of other activities. He was a great gourmet and connoisseur of wines, and he also was very fond of the ladies. He never hid any of these predilections. He was also the best raconteur among pianists, or the best pianist among raconteurs. One story may be quoted here because it concerns a contemporary pianist, whose autograph appears in my collection: Raoul Koczalski. He was a gifted Chopin pianist, though not in the class of Rubinstein. Nevertheless Rubinstein always praised him highly, perhaps because of their common Polish birth and background. One day a mutual friend said to Rubinstein: "You always give such high praise to Koczalski. He does not seem to think highly of you." To which Rubinstein replied: "You know what inveterate liars we both are."

I met Rubinstein once again in the early seventies when he was already an old man. I was attending the music festival in Lucerne where the Chicago Symphony Orchestra under Solti was playing, with Rubinstein as soloist. Late one evening I went back to my hotel, the Schweizerhof, and in the corner of the lobby I found Rubinstein seated with Solti, having a drink. I greeted the gentlemen, and as Solti knew me well, he invited me to join them. I did. I remember there was a third man there whose name I don't recall, whom I didn't know at that time. Solti said "Arthur was complaining about his fading eyesight." At that moment a pretty girl walked through the lobby and Rubinstein's eyes followed her from one end to the other. This was the last impression I had of Arthur Rubinstein. I cannot resist closing with what I think was his wittiest remark. When asked if he ever listened to other pianists, the laconic answer was: "If he plays badly I feel terrible, and if he plays well I feel worse."

Next appears the composer **Béla Bartók** (1881-1945), a frequent visitor to Holland, where he had many friends. Bartók was the first composer of the twentieth century to introduce a strong and sustained rhythmic element in his music and throughout his life never travelled without a metronome for a last check. On the evening of his concert the instrument was sitting on the piano in the soloist's room. Contrary to the way he signs his name in my book, in Hungary he would normally have written Bartók Béla. It is often forgotten that Bartók was as great a pianist as composer and he did give a great many concerts to earn a living. That night he played with his wife Ditta Pasztory, on two pianos. Thanks to impresario De Koos I was allowed to turn the pages for Bartók

Bela Bartok, equally important as composer and pianist.

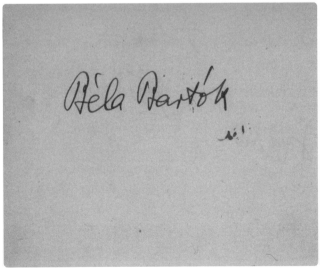

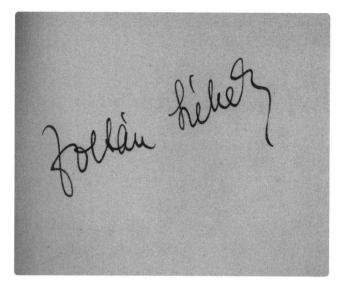

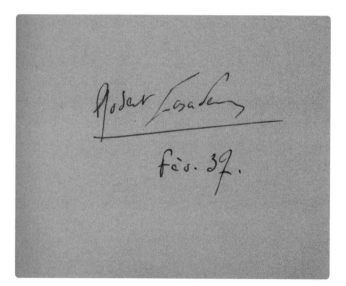

himself. Before the intermission they played Debussy's *En Blanc et Noir* and afterwards Bartók's own Sonata for Two Pianos and Percussion. The percussionists were members of the Concertgebouw Orchestra, Cor Smit and Ton van Dijk. Bartók was a very modest man, and a pleasure to know. In the intermission, when few people came to see us, he asked me if I played the piano, and I said I had practised his early piano pieces. He seemed pleased and said "I'm still very fond of these early works and they brought me close to Romanian and Hungarian folk music." Above is the autograph of **Zoltán Székely** (1903-2001), the Hungarian violinist and close friend of Bartók. He was at the concert, although he did not play that night, but had come simply to accompany Bartók, and I took the opportunity to ask for his autograph. Székely had commissioned

Above: Zoltán Székely, close friend of Béla Bartók and, top left, his autograph.
Bottom left: the autograph of Robert Casadesus, a sensitive and versatile pianist.

the Violin Concerto No. 1 from Bartók, and occasionally consulted him on violin technique. Székely was the primarius of the Hungarian String Quartet which during the War found itself stranded in Holland. The Concertgebouw appointed two of its players, Székely and Koromzay, the violist, as section principals of the orchestra for the duration of the War, but the other two, Moskowski, second violin and Palotai, cello, had a hard time surviving. Székely was soon fired, being Jewish. After the war the quartet emigrated to America and resumed their concert careers. I met Székely once again in Banff in western Canada, where he had retired, although he said he still wanted to play. He explained that his wife, who was Dutch, was very ill, and needed his constant help. And he added: "She has devoted her entire life to me – it's only right that I should attend to her in her remaining years."

Another favourite of mine is **Robert Casadesus** (1899-1972), the French pianist, and the most famous member of a very musical family. I counted six relatives professionally active during his lifetime, excluding his wife Gaby and son Jean, both notable pianists. I met Gaby once when I turned pages for her husband at a chamber music concert. She was born in 1901, and I was delighted to read in The New Yorker that on 22 September 1999 she had attended a special concert in New York in commemoration of the centenary of Robert's birth. In the same year she appeared in a short art film called 'Ravel's Brain', which chronicled the composer's last years. Ravel had been a close friend of Robert and Gaby Casadesus all his life. In fact along with Margérite Long for whom he wrote his piano concerto, Casadesus was Ravel's favourite pianist (*Tombeau de Couperin*). Gaby was a vivacious and articulate lady, who had not lost her touch at the piano. Three months later she died, at the age of ninety-seven. The film was later dedicated to her memory. Casadesus was a very sensitive pianist and had the widest possible range and variety of tone and colour. Interestingly he had thick and stubby fingers and sometimes had difficulty in getting between the black keys. I have come to realise there is no such thing as an ideal pianist's hand.

Oda Slobodskaya (1888-1970) was Russia's best known dramatic soprano, and lived in England from the late 1930s. She was a large lady with a large voice, and when she asked me to show her the concert platform and she saw that it was twenty-five steps down, she said: "I can never manage that up and down several times. I won't go on." This was one of the occasions when the impresario relied on me to find a solution. I went backstage and asked an attendant to show me the work rooms and we found a large standing screen which we brought to the platform and placed in front of the organ only two steps up from the concert area, put a small table and chair behind it, with a glass of water and that was the retreat of Oda Slobodskaya during the performance.

The next autograph is rather special to me. It is that of the pianist **Josef Pembaur,** a surviving pupil of Liszt, along with Lamond and Rosenthal. And thereby hangs a tale.

Olga Slobodskaya, a
large lady and a large
voice.

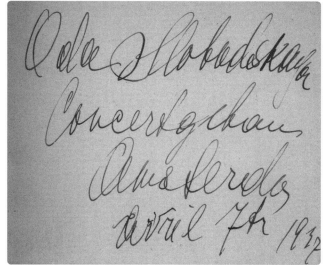

I met Pembaur for the first time after a recital and when I asked him for his autograph he gave me a little morality lesson, favour of Liszt: "Die immer während Betätigung des Ideals ist das Lebens höchster Zweck; zur Erinnerung an den Franz Liszt Abend um dessen Spieler", which translates as "The everlasting pursuit of the Ideal is life's highest purpose. In memory of the Franz Liszt evening and its player." That was a romantic souvenir. To me at sixteen, Pembaur looked ancient, but he was actually not all that old, in fact not yet seventy (he was born in 1875). Although lacking the leonine features of his master, he wore his hair long, from a bald patch in the middle of his head, and as a small man it made him look a bit like a gnome. He was a kind man, with a great deal of physical power - after all, an exclusive Liszt evening is a feat for any pianist.

I turned pages for Pembaur a year later in rather unusual circumstances. Walter Gieseking had been scheduled to play Beethoven's Fourth Piano Concerto with Mengelberg and the Orchestra but had fallen ill at the last moment. In those days, distances were less easy to overcome than they are today, and for practical purposes a substitute had to be found within a hundred miles or so in order for him to be able to come at all, even without a rehearsal. The Concertgebouw also could not ask just anyone to stand in for a famous pianist like Gieseking. Pembaur was found in Brussels (the telephone worked) and he was willing to play, but he said he had not played the concerto in years. Everyone of course wanted to hear him play Liszt, and he was always happy to oblige. So could he please have a page-turner, he asked, and that was where I came in. I was summoned even later, at five o'clock on the day of the concert. When I came to the artist's room, he was seated at the grand piano, studying the score. Mengelberg was nearby putting on his white tie. Pembaur said to me: "I don't need the score for reading. After all I have played the work for the past fifty years, so this is just for reassurance. You turn the pages when I play, I will turn during the orchestral interludes, and if you miss a few pages it doesn't matter." He then turned to Mengelberg and said: "Maestro (conductors are invariably addressed as 'Maestro' – convenient for soloists who forget which day of the week it is and which conductor), I haven't had time to look for a cadenza, let alone practise it, so I will improvise in Liszt's style." He added somewhat patronisingly: "I'll let you know when I come to the end." Mengelberg pulled a long face and asked: "How long do you intend to play?" to which the answer was "about five minutes." Mengelberg commented to me, behind his hand, in Dutch "about four minutes too long."

Mengelberg opened the concert and Pembaur, left alone during this time, sat stock still, as if in a trance. We then went on, and I carried the piano score. When Mengelberg started a work, he always gave a short rap on the music stand which is still audible in the live recordings of the period. On this occasion he gave me a gentle pat on the head with the baton and an encouraging smile. The pianist he politely ignored. It is quite an experience hearing a major symphonic work from the middle of the orchestra, and

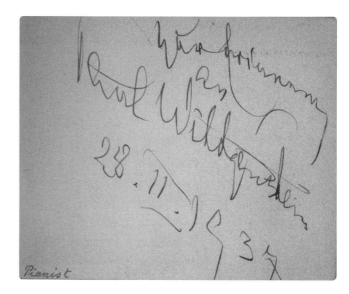

initially I had some problems in hearing individual sections. Pembaur laboured mightily and when the cadenza came, he did indeed improvise, mostly looking at the ceiling for inspiration. When the end came, he motioned with a mighty sweep of his left arm to the orchestra which came in at once. Mengelberg was taken completely by surprise.

'Zur Erinnerung an **Paul Wittgenstein** (1887-1961)' was writtten by the left-handed pianist of the famous Wittgenstein family. His father was a wealthy Austrian industrialist who had five gifted sons. One committed suicide in the early years of this century, two were killed in action during the First World War, Ludwig became the famous philosopher, who taught at Cambridge, one of whose pupils was Maynard Keynes. Before deciding on his vocation Ludwig gave his entire fortune away to his relatives. Paul was the pianist who lost his right arm in the First World War. It did not stop him from attaining international fame and Ravel wrote his *Piano Concerto for the Left Hand* for him with its Danse Macabre atmosphere. This he played at the concert in 1937, when I asked for his autograph (his left-handed writing is quite clear). Other composers who wrote for him were Richard Strauss, Benjamin Britten and Prokofiev.

I would like to talk a little about the next autograph, which is another of my most prized: **Fritz Kreisler** (1875-1962). I also have a photo and a programme of the concert, when I turned pages for his accompanist, my old friend Tasso Janopoulo, the regular partner of Jacques Thibaud. There seems to be a confusion of dates. Although the autograph dates from 1937, the programme is signed 'January 1938' by Kreisler and 'January 1939' by Janopoulos. The latter is obviously a mistake. The 1937 autograph was possibly given after a slightly earlier performance with orchestra, with a musical quotation from a concerto which I cannot remember. On the night of the concert in question, I happened to come early, even slightly before Janopoulo. Kreisler

Left: The autograph of Josef Pembaur, a 19th century style 'piano lion'.
Right: Paul Wittgenstein, a famous pianist and a famous name.

Turning the Pages

Fritz Kreisler, at home
in all types of music;
his autograph and
(following page)
Kreisler on the concert
podium of the
Concergebouw with
Tasso Janopoulo and
the author.

came in a little later. Relaxed as always, he said to Janopoulo and me: "I'm happy to be back in Europe. I've just been to America where they made a terrible fuss." When asked what all the fuss was about, he said: "While in Washington, I decided to go to the Library of Congress, to borrow the manuscript of Brahms' Violin Concerto. You remember (as though either of us were born at that time) that I played it when auditioning for Joseph Joachim, for whom Brahms wrote it, and Brahms was still alive at that time. I'm planning to write a new cadenza. Now, everything kept at the Library of Congress is kept there for eternity. It may not leave the premises, on the penalty of something short of a life sentence. That is why the Budapest String Quartet, when they want to make a recording, on the four fabulous Stradivarius instruments, have to come to the Library, and not the instruments to them. The librarian looked at me and seemed to recognise me, at least he said "at risk of penalty, I will lend you the manuscript, but be sure to return it to me within a few days." Later, when I was in New York, and had finished with the score, I wrapped it in brown paper and mailed it back to the Library. They received it in good order, but then all hell broke loose: "How did I dare send such a uniquely valuable manuscript in the mail? Suppose it had been lost? If you had called, we could have come to fetch it!" I didn't know what all the fuss was about. I send my own music in the mail all the time."

Incidentally, Brahms himself was known to have sent the manuscript of his Fourth Symphony by parcel post, when no copy yet existed. Von Bülow is the reliable source of that story. Janopoulo and I looked at each other and mouthed one word: typical. During the intermission the Chairman of the Concertgebouw, Dr. H. P. Heineken (of Heineken's beer) happened to walk in. Dr. Heineken was an amateur pianist of above average talent, who occasionally played with the orchestra (I suppose without a fee), at Cecilia pension fund benefits, for example. Dr. Heineken knew Kreisler well and they started an animated conversation, during which I heard the following story. Kreisler recalled that he had visited Antonin Dvořák in 1903 (the year before his death) at his impoverished home in Prague: "Dvořák was lying in bed, sick and in visibly bad shape. He had sold all his compositions for a pittance and had barely anything to live on. Even the emoluments of his brilliant American tour had been used up. I had been playing some of his Slavonic Dances and was visiting in order to pay my respects to the old man. I asked him if he had anything more for me to play. "Look through that pile," the sick composer said, pointing to a heap of unorganized papers. "Maybe you can find something." I did, and found the Humoresque." It was, of course, Kreisler who subsequently arranged this piece and made it world famous through playing it in recital. Thinking of this now, it is probably an apocryphal story, but Kreisler no doubt dined out on it for many years. Incidentally, Dr Heineken was a staunch anti-Nazi and when he was forced to shake hands during the war with Seyss Inquart, the Austrian Nazi Governor of Holland, at a Concertgebouw reception, he was heard to say quite loudly

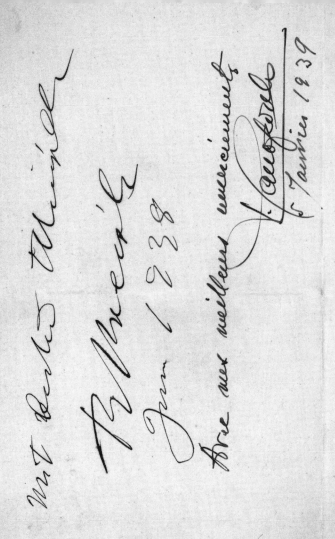

PROGRAMMA

1. **SONATE** Op. 30, No. 3, G gr. t. . L. v. Beethoven
   Allegro assai.   (1770—1827)
   Tempo di Minuetto.
   Allegro Vivace..

2. **CIACONNA** uit de Partita in d kl. t. . J. S. Bach
                                                     (1685— 1750)

3. **CONCERTO** No. 22, in a kl. t. . J. B. Viotti
   Allegro.   (1753 – 1824)
   Andante.
   Finale.

PAUZE

4. **ROMANZE** F gr. t., Op. 50 . L. van Beethoven

5. **RONDO** G gr. t. . . . . W. A. Mozart
                                                     (1756—1791)

6. **RONDO** D gr. t. . . . . F. Schubert
                                                     (1797—1828)

7. **SCHERZO**. . . . . P. Tschaikowsky
                                                     (1840 – 1893)

Begeleiding: TASSO JANOPOULO.

Concertvleugel: STEINWAY & SONS.

"Now I have to wash my hands." Soon afterwards he was forced to step down from the Board.

When you look at the programme of Kreisler's 1938 concert, which included the Violin Concerto No. 22 of Viotti and the Bach Chaconne, taken out of the Partita, you are seeing an example of the traditional old-fashioned format, dedicated in German and French. In the intermission of this concert, Kreisler turned to me and said: "I suppose I will have to play one of my own encores. Which would you like to hear – 'Liebesleid' or 'Liebesfreud'?" Cheeky young lad that I was, I answered: "Both, if you please." I got both. To hear him play 'Liebesfreud' makes you understand why Menuhin once said that he locked himself in a hotel room for several hours with a Kreisler recording, in order to try to get the rubato right. I shall never forget this marvellous classical violinist with a Viennese lilt, who was then sixty three years old. Eventually we even got *Schön Rosmarin*,

The programme played at the concert where the author turned the pages, with dedication.

Turning the Pages

Nathan Milstein. His autograph bears an inscription from Brahms' *Violin Concerto.*

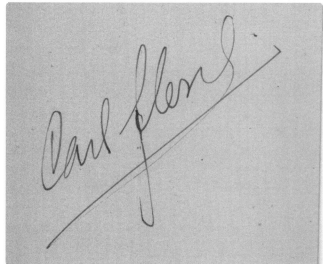

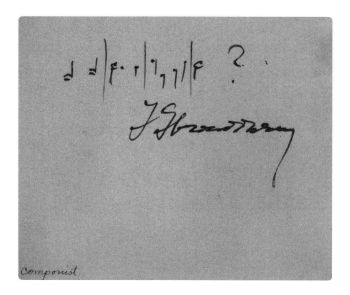

Componist

Top left: the autograph of Leopold Mittman, Milstein's
accompanist at the concert where I turned the pages.
Below left: Igor Stravinsky's autograph with the Jeu des Cartes
motif and (right) Stravinsky with Pierre Monteux.
Top right: the autograph of Carl Flesch, a legend among violin
pedagogues.

which is the essential Viennese Kreisler. Neither his compositions, nor his playing, nor even the cadenzas he wrote for the Beethoven Concerto have been forgotten.

Nathan Milstein (1904-1992), the Russian-born violinist, lived in America, but toured the world. His autograph has a dedication and a few bars from Brahms' Violin Concerto. Milstein played regularly in Amsterdam with his partner Leopold Mittmann. Whenever I went to turn pages at his concerts, half an hour or so before starting time, Milstein would be there in the soloist's room, fiddling away, working at a new fingering or bowing, in order to improve his beloved 'clarity'. Indeed, he was famous for that quality. After the War, I met him in the early sixties in Philadelphia where he was giving a concert. I went backstage and he seemed pleased to see me. He said: "I must introduce you to my pianist, but he only speaks Russian and Polish and I chose him partly for that reason, because otherwise he is so good he would be pinched by someone else." He had an aversion to flying and did all his travelling by car, train or boat. That is until I met him much later by chance, I think in the late seventies, in the lobby of a hotel in Geneva. He beckoned me over and said "You might be interested to know that next week I am playing in Tokyo." I said: "How do you expect to get there?" He said: "Oh, I have got over my fear of flying – a bit late in the day, but there it is."

The next autograph is also of a violinist, **Carl Flesch** (1873-1944), a well known concert violinist in his day, but even better known as a violin pedagogue. He was a teacher of many outstanding violinists of his generation and the next one, and he travelled in his early years extensively. He considered Szymon Goldberg one of his best pupils. He moved for a while to live in The Hague, where he married a Dutch lady. When I turned the pages for him his wife came along and we all spoke Dutch. He never quite lost his accent. He is still remembered today by performing musicians for his *Carl Flesch Violin Method*. A few years ago, when visiting London, I met his son, Carl F. Flesch, who had become an insurance broker. He had written a biography of his father, but rather from his own point of view, because his father's friends and almost everybody else always asked when they met him: "And do you also play the violin?" This became the title of his memoir, first published in German. When I started these recollections, I thought of the first question Lili Kraus put to me after I had asked for her autograph: "Do you read music too?"

Now comes **Igor Stravinsky** (1882-1971). Stravinsky was a friend of Mengelberg, who championed his music regularly and to whom Stravinsky dedicated some of his works. At this particular concert, when I asked for his autograph, he looked at me and said: "I will write a motif in your book. If you can answer where it comes from I will sign it. If not, you will have to make do with the motif." I gave him the answer: *Jeu de Cartes* and with a smile and a flourish he signed my book.

Alfred Cortot (1877-1962), the French pianist, appears in this book with the opening bars of a Chopin mazurka. With his frail build, deep-set eyes and his long hair

Alfred Cortot, a man for all seasons.

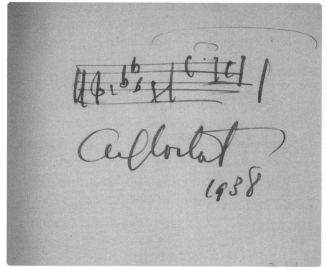

parted in the middle, he looked the original Romantic pianist. He was one of the most gifted musicians of the 19th and 20th centuries, a natural talent that absorbed all music almost as casually as he ate and drank. It was said that in his twenties he could play any part of a Wagner opera by heart. That is hard to check today but it is a fact that between 1902 and 1904 he conducted the Paris première of *Tristan und Isolde* and a few years later the same of Beethoven's *Missa Solemnis*, Brahms' *Deutsches Requiem*, *Götterdämmerung* and *Parsifal*. It is incredible to think that that these masterworks had not been performed before in Paris. Later in life he gave up conducting. He had a great virtuosity as a pianist, which he always considered as a means to an end. He recorded at a time when cutting and slicing was rare, so most of his recordings were made in one take. When he played a wrong note, which was fairly frequently, he was asked to re-play the piece, to which he invariably replied "Leave it. It shows I am human." He wrote several books and did a new edition of all Chopin works. In fact he was considered the Chopin player of his time who resembled Chopin most closely. Today pianists like Alfred Brendel have great admiration for him. At the first recital of his that I heard, he played all the Chopin Préludes. He also contributed his own programme notes, in which he associated each Prélude with a colour which in his mind defined the work. In a similar way, Brendel, forty years later, gave each of Beethoven's Diabelli Variations its own sub-title.

I had the pleasure of turning pages for Cortot only once, in 1938, when he played with his famous trio – the Cortot, Thibaud Casals Trio, but on this occasion Fournier had replaced Casals. During the intermission, when no one was allowed in the soloists' room, they let me stay. Thibaud smoked his innumerable cigarettes and Cortot was in a talkative mood. He asked me "Do you play the piano?" and I answered that I was just then studying his edition of the Chopin Mazurkas, which seemed to please him (hence his dedication). This emboldened me to ask for advice on rubato playing. He was silent and then said "think of a tree, firmly rooted in the earth, but its branches swaying with the wind. So it is with rubato piano playing. The left hand is firm, the right hand plays freely with the mood of the music." I will never forget this. For some reason he also commented on his teacher, the pianist Raoul Pugno, the mid 19th –century pianist who played as répétiteur for Wagner at his opera rehearsals. He could memorise a score simply by reading it, during a train ride from, say, Berlin to Munich. All he had to do, according to Cortot, was to sit on the score during the concert. Again, *se non è vero...* Cortot also acted as a sort of cultural delegate for the French government for a number of years. He died in his nineties, leaving a large treasure of souvenirs behind and an equally large number of pupils, Clara Haskil, Monique Haas, Janine Weil, Jacques Février, not forgetting Yvonne Lefébure. But there was only one pupil he called "perfect", and that was Dinu Lipatti.

Now comes one of my small treasures: **Serge Rachmaninoff** (1873-1943). I heard him in recital – one of his rare recitals in Holland. He was an imposing figure, at least

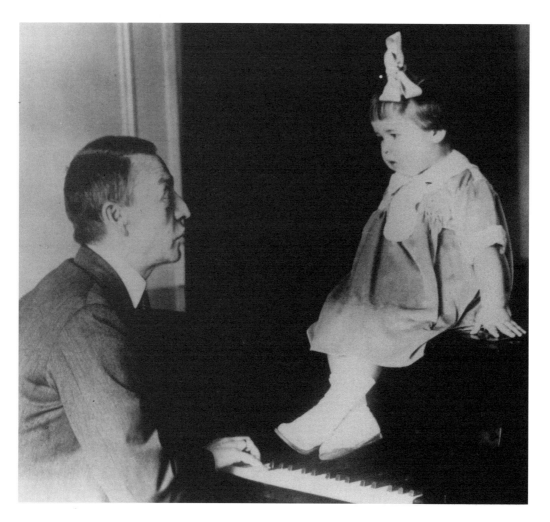

Left and below left:
Serge Rachaninioff, a
legend in his time and
his autograph.
Below right: the
autograph of Moura
Lympany, a favourite of
the public of her time.
She signed with her
real name.

Pianist-componist

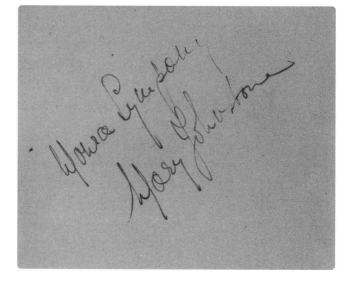

Turning the Pages

six feet four inches tall, gaunt-looking and unsmiling, with close-cropped hair and large hands which could span more than an octave. As an encore he had just thundered his way through the popular C sharp minor Prelude, which he had composed while still a student. Its instant popularity came to haunt him and he used to be asked for it so often that he would refer to it as 'it' and would tease audiences by pretending he did not know what they were asking for. After the concert I went to the Soloists' Room, where a guard had been posted to keep people out. Of course the guard knew me and I was in in a second. Rachmaninoff was known never to indulge autograph hunters. He was alone in the room with Mengelberg, who had attended the concert. Rachmaninoff had just told him that he had premiered his Third Piano Concerto in 1910 in New York with Gustav Mahler conducting. Rachmaninoff's first concert in Holland took place in 1903 when he played his Second Piano Concerto with Mengelberg conducting. For a young boy these were magical moments. He was still disinclined to give an autograph, but Mengelberg introduced me as the 'house cat' of the Concertgebouw, since I could be found anywhere in the building. After that Rachmaninoff gave me his autograph with a rare smile.

The following signature is a bit of a curiosity: the English pianist **Moura Lympany**, very well-known in her day and a favourite of Mengelberg as soloist. I asked for her autograph before the concert and I do not know why I mentioned it - Moura Lympany was her stage name and I knew her real name was Mary Johnstone. So I asked her to sign her real name below and she smiled and signed 'Mary Johnstone'.

Late in 1938 an event took place which was very special to me – my first opera. Amsterdam in those days had no opera house, and in the twenties some prosperous citizens founded a society for the purpose of bringing opera to Amsterdam in a very exclusive way - no more than two performances per year, but of the highest calibre. They called this venture the Wagner Society. Membership was expensive and tickets even more so. All events were black tie. My father had become a member in the thirties. The society set its sights high. I remember seeing programmes – not the performances - of Erich Kleiber, with the entire Berlin opera performing *Lohengrin*, the Paris Opera performing Dukas' *Ariane et Barbe Bleu*, Václav Talich and the Prague Opera doing Smetana's *Bartered Bride* (*Prodana Nevesta*), and then in the autumn of 1938 the most perfect opera ever written: Mozart's *Nozze di Figaro*, sung in Italian. Incidentally, the Concertgebouw Orchestra was always in the pit.

The cast of *Figaro* was taken from a Salzburg performance some years earlier and was superb. **Mariano Stabile** (1888-1968) was Figaro. He was famous as Toscanini's Falstaff. **Tancredi Pasero** (1893-1983) was the Count – both singers were the top singers at La Scala and sang at the re-opening of that house, conducted by Toscanini in 1946. The Finnish soprano, **Aulikki Rautavaara** was the Countess, courtesy of the Glyndebourne opera. **Margit Bokor**, from Vienna, was Susanna, and **Jarmila Novotná** (1907-1984),

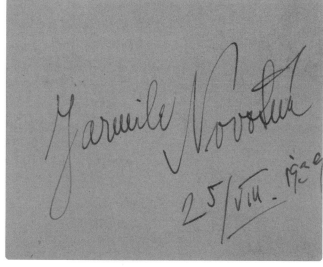

Above, left: Jarmila
Novotna, then and
now one of my
favourite singers and,
right, her autograph.
Below, left: Mariano
Stabile, a favourite
singer of Toscanini.
His autograph is on
the opposite page.

Opposite page
autographs clockwise
from top left: Pasero
Tancredi, a marvellous
opera singer with
acting ability;
Mariano Stabile;
Aulikki Rautavaara,
one of the few
prominent singers of
her country, Finland;
Margit Bokor, a
seasoned member of
the Vienna State
Opera.

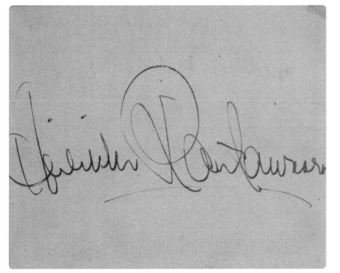

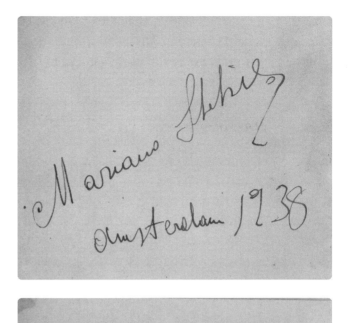

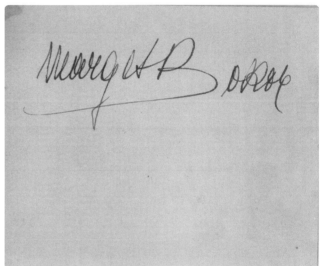

also from Vienna, as Cherubino. The conductor was Bruno Walter, who accompanied the recitatives himself at the piano. I did of course not attend the performance, but I got into the dress rehearsal. The hall was empty and it felt like a private performance. The music was superbly performed as behoved the reputation of the singers, orchestra and conductor but even my inexperienced eye could see that the acting left much to be desired. On the stage there was at times more commotion than motion, at other times singers stood stock still, occasionally raising an arm. That is, until Cherubino appeared. A slim girl, in a close-fitting 18th century court uniform, the Czech-Austrian singer Jarmila Novotná, doing the famous trouser role. She literally radiated and dominated the entire scene with her vivid and natural acting, and when she opened her mouth the perfection was total. No wonder. As a young girl she was coached as an actress by Max Reinhardt, the founder of the Salzburg Festival, and acted in *A Midsummer Night's Dream* and other plays. Soon someone discovered she had a voice. She took singing lessons and became the ideal of every opera director: the singer who could act. It was perhaps a bit unfair to the rest of the cast. For me, the entire performance was and is unforgettable. All autographs appear in my book. This was 1938, and we were promised *Don Giovanni* for 1939. This never came to pass because of the war, although it was still the so-called 'phoney' war – nothing happened in Holland until May 1940. Incidentally, the year written under Jarmila Novotná's autograph, 1939, is a mistake. It should be 1938.

I lost track of Jarmila Novotná although I knew she had managed to escape to America. Then in the early eighties I was on one of my regular visits to the Salzburg Festival and went to the photographic exhibition two lady musicologists arranged yearly on the occasion of the Festival. This was in the Arensberg Palace, which is not really a palace but a large mansion. There had previously been exhibitions of photographs of Reinhardt, Hofmannsthal, and Stefan Zweig, and this year's focus was on the early Salzburg years - the 1920s and 1930s. There suddenly Jarmila Novotná leapt off the wall, first as an actress in her twenties and then as Cherubino, Pamina, Octavia and others. I was fascinated. The organising ladies were present and I went to ask them if they knew what had happened to Jarmila Novotná. In a matter of fact way they said, "Oh, she was here yesterday, looking well. She is in her seventies, widowed and living in Vienna." I asked if they had her address and one of them said, "Yes, but we are not supposed to give it to strangers." The other interrupted: "But we have known this gentleman for several years." I asssured them that I had no intention of gatecrashing on her; in fact I had to return the next day to Zürich. Very ceremoniously they gave me her address.

The next day alone in my hotel room in Zürich, I decided to write to her. Forty-five years had passed since I heard her, and I could only repeat the impression she had made on me at that time. I mentioned of course my visit the previous day to Salzburg. Within a week I had a letter back. She was very moved by my words, so long after the event, which she remembered well, and said she had not received such letters in many years. She filled me in on the intervening years. In America she had continued at the Metropolitan Opera, sang recitals and also made a few films, *Die Fledermaus* amongst others. After the war she had returned to Vienna and became a member of the Staatsoper. Soon, however, she married, an Austrian Count - she didn't mention his title, but I found out later – who was general manager of the IBM Corporation in Austria. When her two sons were born she soon stopped singing. She was then in her early forties. Her husband had died years ago, her sons were grown up and lived in the United States, which she visited yearly. In closing, she asked me to come and visit her when I was in Vienna and said she would take me to her favourite restaurant.

It was not until ten years later that my wife and I revisited Vienna to hear Placido Domingo. When strolling along the Kärtnerstrasse, I passed a small shop window with photos of Vienna's pre-war musical days, even pre-World War I. It was no more than a hole in the wall, such as you would only find in Vienna or Salzburg. I had of course been thinking of Jarmila Novotná, but somehow had lost or forgotten or mislaid her letter and therefore didn't have her address. I walked into the shop and somewhat hesitatingly asked the old lady behind the counter if she had any photos of Jarmila Novotná. She did not hesitate at all and said, "Yes, give me a moment." Literally, out of a shoe box appeared a few minutes later a postcard-photograph of Jarmila Novotná. The photograph was dedicated to a personal friend of hers, thirty years earlier, but the photo itself was from the 1940s. It showed a pleasant oval face, with regular features and the hairdo of the 1940s. A pretty young lady, but not a star; that she became only on stage. I could not help asking the lady if she knew what had become of her and she said she had died the previous year in her mid-eighties. So ten years before, I had missed her by a day in Salzburg and now I had missed her by a year in Vienna. I paid the old lady a small sum of money for the photo and left the shop with it, feeling saddened by these missed opportunities.

Yehudi Menuhin and his accompanist Henk Endt, with the author turning the pages.

The young Yehudi Menuhin and
even younger Hephzibah

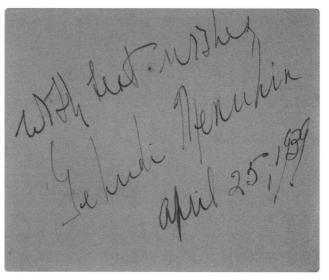

I now come to another special autograph with a dedication, that of **Yehudi Menuhin** (1916-1999). Yehudi was, of course, the unsurpassed prodigy of hs time, but his sisters, Hepzibah and Yaltah were scarcely less gifted. Hepzibah gave her first public recital at the age of eight in 1928, when she played Bach's Italian Concerto. Her father Moshe decided that his daughters would not be given the same education and privileges as Yehudi, however. His view was that "One prodigy in the family is enough." In 1938 I turned pages for Menuhin's accompanist Henk Endt, a Dutch pianist. I have a photograph taken at this concert. Note how high Yehudi holds his violin, facilitating his marvellously smooth bowing technique. After the concert Yehudi told me he was getting married in London the following week. He was going to marry the Australian heiress Nola Nolan, a sporting extrovert beauty. Yehudi's parents, who were non-religious and, of course, non-Zionist, considered her a suitable partner because she was a "non-Jewish Australian girl and therefore exotic as well as rich, and built for childbearing." Indeed two children emerged soon: Zamira and Krov. Hephzibah also jumped at the chance to escape her dedicated but authoritarian parents to marry the handsome brother of Yehudi's bride for a new life on his 32,000 acre sheep farm. The first thing she did when setting sail for Australia was to throw overboard a bundle of cruelly boned corsets.

Yehudi and Hephzibah returned to Amsterdam for a sonata evening, as a last rehearsal for a recording session in London. Hephzibah was a totally equal partner for her brother, witness their performance of Beethoven's Kreutzer Sonata, of which a recording exists. What a beautiful pianist she was, frail Hephzibah, just a year older than myself. When I told her in the interval that in France during my summer vacation I had heard her teacher Marcel Ciampi, she was delighted and it established a bond between us. She told me she had had long sessions with Ciampi, sometimes together with Yehudi's teacher, the Romanian-born violinist and composer George Enescu. She showed me a photograph of the four of them together.

Predictably both Yehudi's and Hephzibah's marriages were a disaster. Yehudi used to refer to his as a ghastly "mistake." He married his Diana in 1947. Hephzibah also remarried and re-emerged as Yehudi's partner in the same year, but also devoted her time to a centre for sick and homeless people in south London, thus putting into practice the humanitarian ideas shared by all the Menuhin children. I never saw Hepzibah again. She died in 1981. I met Yehudi again in the nineteen seventies, when he visited Hong Kong with Diana, following a concert and a teaching tour of China. He did not play in Hong Kong on that visit. The other sister Yaltah vanished from the public eye. Imagine my surprise when she re-appeared with three spoken sentences in a BBC memorial programme after Yehudi's death in 1999.

Yehudi's wide range of interests is well known and included a taste for adventure and the good things in life. On his own initiative he organised and gave the first concert after the liberation at the Paris Opéra, which included the Mendelssohn Concerto (forbidden by the German occupiers), Lalo's Symphonie Espagnole and the Beethoven Concerto. It was a matinee performance and waiting anxiously in the wings and trying to restrain the encores was the pilot who had to fly Yehudi back to London and whose plane was not equipped for night flying. An American jeep took them to Le Bourget, only for the plane's electrical system to fail over the Channel. There was a forced landing in Kent. Undismayed, Yehudi caught a local bus and train to London. In his double violin case a Reblochon cheese, some French perfume and a bottle of Champagne also made it safely across the Channel. Yehudi's generosity to deserving and non-deserving causes is proverbial, but he had a good sense of his own worth. He always instructed his agents that no violinist should be paid more than himself.

The photograph I mentioned earlier was in a way a special one, and was taken by Dr Erich Salomon. Salomon was born in Berlin, from a well-to-do family, and had studied law. When he came out of the First World War his father's fortune had evaporated in the financial disaster of Germany in the 1920s and he decided to make a profession of his photography hobby. He became the photographer of the *Berliner Illustrierter*, the two million circulation weekly and soon became known as the king of indiscretion. In fact he was the first *paparazzo*. One of his celebrated pictures was taken at the Second Peace Conference in The Hague in 1930, where Germany tried to re-negotiate its war reparation payments. He borrowed a ladder from the fire brigade and took a picture through the window of the hotel of the tuxedoed delegates napping in different postures in their chairs. He also photographed Marlene Dietrich, still in Germany, in her bed!

In 1933, when Hitler came to power, he happened to be in Holland, where his wife was born and he stayed there. The photograph of Menuhin in concert was no indiscretion. He placed his large Ermanox tripod camera at the end of the balcony, facing the platform, and took his picture without a flash. By then he had become the first photographer in the world who copyrighted his pictures so that no one could use them without payment. His law degree had no doubt something to do with that. When I asked him if I could have a copy, he said: "Young man, I am not in the habit of giving pictures away, but since you are in it, I suppose I could make an exception." He even framed it for me and on the back wrote: "This picture may not be used for publication without my explicit consent. Dr. Erich Salomon." While Salomon remained in Holland, his colleagues and competitors went elsewhere to great fame – Alfred Eisenstadt to the U.S., where he joined Life magazine, André Friedman to Paris, where he changed his name to Robert Capa and founded the famous Magnum studio and Tim Gidal to London for *Picture Post*. They were all of course Jews and that meant that Germany was practically left without good professional photographers apart from Leni Riefenstahl, who was Hitler's personal favourite. During the war, Salomon walked into an SS trap and was sent to Auschwitz where he died with his wife and second son. I heard this story from his eldest son, who went to England, joined the British army during the War, changed his name to Peter Hunter to avoid the Nazis and became an insurance broker.

I met Menuhin more than forty years later, when he and Diana were on a visit to Hong Kong. He played, although the tremor in his arm was noticeable. Soon he stopped performing altogether and concentrated on conducting. Menuhin passed away recently and much has been and is being written about his kindness, his universality (playing in Germany with Furtwängler after the war, for example), his sincerity, his loyalty to friends and his generosity. It is all perfectly true. For me he was for the first thirty performing years of his life the most outstanding violinist of the last century. Technique and depth of understanding and power of expression went hand in hand. His autograph and photo help to remind me of this, if reminding were necessary. My meetings with him and his sister Hepzibah have enriched my life.

Claudio Arrau (1903-1991) was born in Chili and a true child prodigy. He played for the first time before an audience at the age of five and at seven was accepted at the Santiago Conservatory. Before the First World War he was sent to Berlin to study with Martin Krauser, himself a former pupil of Liszt. He had the technique and an infallible memory. Although, with his smooth black hair and thin moustache, he looked a bit like the latin lover, he was a serious and shy young man, who suffered terrible bouts of nerves before a concert. He then did something unusual in those days: he consulted a psychiatrist and was eventually cured of his nervous condition. When Cortot heard him at the 1927 Geneva Competition he was impressed: "Voilà un pianiste!"

Soon he turned to the classical repertoire and in 1935 was the first pianist to play all Bach's piano works publicly. His range of works comprised the entire piano repertoire. He played an average of 120 concerts per year and recorded widely. I recommend (specially for Dutch readers) Beethoven's Fourth Piano Concerto with the Concertgebouw Orchestra under Eduard van Beinum, recorded in 1959, the year of the conductor's death. Martha Argerich says that Arrau's playing of the Andante was one of her most moving experiences.

I mentioned earlier Arrau's high state of nervousness before a concert. The same Martha Argerich says that she loves playing the piano, but hates being a pianist. She suffered several bouts of depression, a serious one at the age of 22 or 23, just before she won the Warsaw Chopin Competition in 1965. She hated being alone on the podium and hasn't given a solo recital in years. She prefers chamber music and works with orchestra. She recently said that she will try again to give solo recitals or at least 'half a recital'.

The autograph of the French violinist **Jacques Thibaud** (1880-1953) was given to me after a concert - the first of many - at which I turned pages for his accompanist. He was the very image of the proverbial Frenchman, who had a sometimes deceptive air of nonchalance, great flair and a cavalier attitude to life. He spoke only French, but in

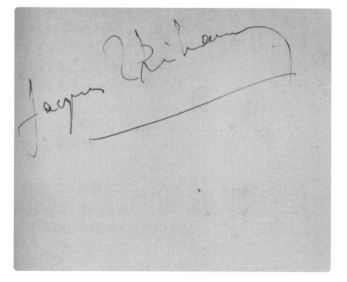

that language he was a brilliant causeur, talking incessantly but intelligently. He also played preferably French music. At a subscription concert he played in two consecutive years Lalo's Symphonie Espagnole, a work rarely performed in concert today. His recital programmes were in 19th-century style, also preferably French. He was born in 1880 and had started his career as a prodigy. As a programme example, he would play a violin concerto with piano accompaniment by, for instance, his beloved Lalo or Wienawski. After the intermission, short pieces and fireworks. Occasionally the concerto would be replaced by a sonata - by César Franck or Guillaume Lekeu. He was usually accompanied by the Greek pianist Tasso Janopoulo, who also sometimes played with Kreisler.

At one of Thibaud's concerts I went early to the soloist's room and found him pacing the room diagonally, his usual cigarette dangling from the corner of his mouth and walking from one end of the room to the other. In one corner was a grand piano, in the other a small table, both with ashtrays, in which he flicked his ash from time to time. Through the smoke he looked at me, or rather peered at me suspiciously. In another corner was Tasso Janopoulo, seated rather despondently. He beckoned me over and said, "We are heading for a small disaster. Thibaud has got it into his head to start the programme with Beethoven's Kreutzer Sonata. Now we know that Thibaud needs about five to ten minutes to find his intonation, after which of course he is perfect. So I don't know what will happen tonight when he starts the sonata with the solo chords." There was not much we could do about it at that stage so we went on. Thibaud took five minutes to tune his violin, which he had done elaborately in the soloist's room and then started on the Kreutzer Sonata, indeed, fully a half tone below pitch. When Janopoulo came in with the piano, everybody winced. Thibaud didn't seem to notice and ten minutes later he played like a god throughout the evening.

I read the other day that three young musicians in Berlin have founded a Jacques Thibaud String Trio, and are exceptional for playing all their concerts by heart It's nice to know that forty years after his death, a performing musician is remembered in this way. Thibaud would have been amused. The only trio he ever played in was the Cortot/Thibaud/Casals Piano Trio. How the young Berliners knew that indeed Thibaud had a healthy disregard for written music on the concert platform, if he could help it, I do not know.

Since my own 'career' took place at the piano at the Concertgebouw, this may be the right moment to mention the most important Dutch piano accompanists (the term usually used before the war) for whom I regularly turned pages. **Marinus Flipse** (1908-1997) was one of them. A characteristic they all shared was total unflappability in the face of unexpected crises, and competence in foreign languages. Both were very necessary, bearing in mind the nervousness of artists before and sometimes during or even after a concert. Flipse was also a chamber music player but rarely did solo work.

Opposite page left: Claudio Arrau, a true child prodigy who was accepted at the Santiago Conservatory when he was seven. Right: Jacques Thibaud. His recital programmes were in the 19th century style, preferably French.

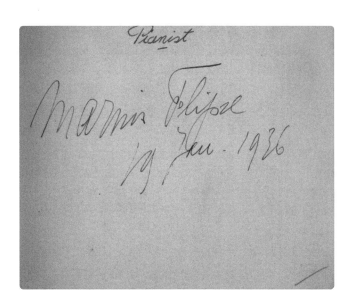

Pianist

Marinus Flipse
19 Jan. 1936

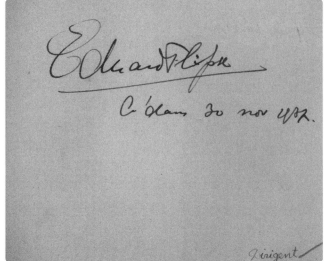

Eduard Flipse
Coblens 30 nov 48?.

Dirigent

Turning the Pages

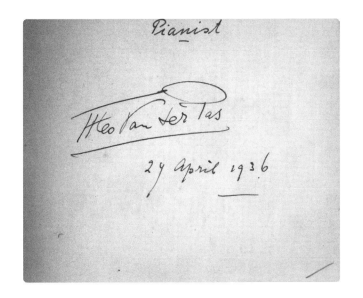

Theo van der Pas (1902-1986) was purely an accompanist, but of the calibre of Rudolf Jansen today. He was always impeccably dressed and groomed and the most unflappable, even phlegmatic, of all. He was always available and therefore the most sought-after by impresarios. For some reason he became fond of me and always let me know when my services were required. One day he rang to ask me if I could assist him at a concert in a hotel outside Amsterdam, the Hamdorf Hotel in Laren (well-known to older readers, it was torn down many years ago). That posed a small problem, because van der Pas lived in The Hague, and could not come by to fetch me in his car. Finally I went by train and bus and stayed overnight at the Hamdorf. All this van der Pas paid for, as well as the excellent dinner we had together. That is the way to get to know your artists!

Felix de Nobel (1907-1981) was my favourite accompanying pianist, and someone who became a friend. He was a multi-talented artist. When a soprano was not on top form, he managed to transpose her songs by one or two tones while sight-reading. He was also founder and conductor of the Netherlands Chamber Choir, a small group of selected professional singers, for which he chose, and where necessary adapted, an uncommonly fascinating repertoire. He did the same thing with Harry van Os, a well-known singer, who more aptly could be called a modern troubadour, and who had a worldwide repertoire of folk songs, for which Felix wrote an always original and usually witty accompaniment. Those were special evenings, and they included a certain measure of improvisation which always went down well with the audience. Felix de Nobel toured the entire country both with his choir and with Harry van Os. He was also adept at four-handed piano concerts with Marinus Flipse (remember the extensive Schubert repertoire for this combination). Both were great football fans, albeit for different clubs, and when the time came for me to turn a page, and I had to reach across the entire keyboard, one of them would whisper to me: "pass across the field" ("over de hele").

Felix lived near my home in the southern part of Amsterdam and I would visit him regularly. I learned a great deal from him about music and how to be happy in a life of music. One day we were talking about Berlioz and Felix said of him: "No great friend of mine — he is larger than life," which was something he disliked instinctively. I also got to know his charming wife Dora — Doortje to us. She had an attractive soprano voice and appeared successfully in soubrette roles on the stage in Holland and abroad. It was also an amusing coincidence that my mother and Doortje became friends by buying bread at the same corner bakery.

Having praised these pre-war accompanying pianists, as they were called, I must mention in the same breath a living piano partner of many singers: **Rudolf Jansen**. He belongs to the class of pianists which emerged more than sixty years ago with Gerald Moore, and his first claim to fame was as partner to Elly Ameling, with whom he travelled world-wide. He has since moved from strength to strength. To hear this self-effacing man today with an artist like Robert Holl, another famous Dutch, or rather international, singer, is a revelation. No wonder he is in growing demand as partner and voice coach by young and not so young singers today.

2

Other Musicians at the Concertgebouw 1934-1940

The stories in the previous chapter have, I hope, made for easy reading, and for that reason I did not want to interrupt them by including autographs more suitable for browsing rather than reading in sequence. The latter nevertheless form the bulk of my collection, and are reminders of a now closed past. I hope that my readers will come across some happy memories.

Emanuel Feuermann (1902-1942) the cellist was born in Galicia, and was one of the greatest musical prodigies of the 20th century. He was made a conservatory professor at the age of 16. He was a cellist's cellist; colleagues tend to prefer him to the more famous - but also more idiosyncratic - Pablo Casals. He all but created the modern cello sound. Having moved to Austria to avoid the Nazis, Feuermann was on the verge of stardom whe he died at the age of 39, in 1942.

The renowned bass **Alexander Kipnis** (1891-1978), from Russia, was well known as a recitalist as well as an opera singer. He sang at the Metropolitan Opera during the war.

Frederic Lamond (1868-1948) was born in 1868 in Scotland but lived most of his life in Berlin. He was a pupil of Liszt, and specialized in Beethoven. I heard him play Beethoven's 5th Piano Concerto, the 'Emperor', in the nineteen thirties. He was a small man, who sat hunched over the keyboard as he played. He gave his signature after the concert, hence his words "Zur freundlichen Erinnerung" (in kind memory). He was one of the few living artists who had attended Tchaikovsky's funeral in St Petersburg in 1893, and enjoyed reminiscing about it.

Walter Gieseking (1895-1956), with Backhaus and Wilhelm Kempff, was one of the great German pianists of his time. He was a large man, playing Beethoven with an amazing force and a great subtlety in Debussy. In fact, considering all other interpretations on record, his name was almost synonymous with that of Debussy, as Schnabel's was with Beethoven and Rubinstein's with Chopin. With regard to his acknowledged

Top and centre left:
Emmanuel Feuermann.
Top and centre right:
Walter Gieseking.
Bottom left;
Alexander Kipnis.
Bottom right:
Frederic Lamond

Cellist.

Emanuel Feuermann

24. Nov. 35

Amsterdam

Pianist

Walter Gieseking

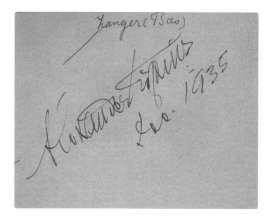

Zanger (Bas)

Alexander Kipnis
Dec. 1935

Pianist.

Zur freundlichen
Erinnerung

Frederic Lamond

26.12-35

Turning the Pages

affinity with Debussy, it is interesting to note that he was actually born in Lyon, France, where his father practised medicine, but moved to Germany at the age of sixteen. He was no doubt sympathetic to the Nazi movement, but was not an active supporter like von Karajan. In 1945 Gieseking was allowed to play for the Occupation Forces in the American zone in Germany. Later in the year, however, he was banned by the American Military Government. Britain, France and Austria objected to this ban. After thorough investigation the ban was lifted a year later, and he was cleared by a Denazification Court. A Carnegie Hall concert had to be cancelled in 1949 because of disturbances, but he was unconditionally accepted in America four years later. He toured the world, talking of a new dawn for Germany but tried to veto Emil Gilels getting first prize in Brussels because he was Jewish.

Ernest Ansermet (1883-1969), was a Swiss conductor who studied and taught mathematics before founding the Orchestre de la Suisse Romande, in Geneva in 1918. He always was a great champion of new music and a friend of Ravel, Roussel and Stravinsky.

Georg Széll (1897-1970), the famous Hungarian conductor and pianist, was known in his time as a great orchestra builder, first in Prague, where he started his career, but he also left his mark on all the orchestras he conducted in Europe, before emigrating to the United States. He was appointed chief conductor of the Cleveland Orchestra, which he turned into an orchestra on a par with Boston and Philadelphia. He was hated by most orchestral musicians for his disciplinarian behaviour and bad temper, but he nevertheless extracted the best from them, and he therefore had their respect. Even today, the Cleveland Orchestra's former conductor, Christoph von Dohnányi, says "When I have a bad night, it's my fault, when I have a good night, Georg Széll gets the credit." In Szell's defence, his friends used to say that he was his own worst enemy, to which Rudolf Bing, the General Manager of the Metropolitan Opera said "not as long as I am alive!"

The following entry needs no introduction – **Bruno Walter** (1876-1962), the disciple and friend of Mahler. And as Mahler said, "together with Mengelberg, they are the best interpreters of my works." He was also a distinguished pianist, who used to give recitals with Lotte Lehmann, Elizabeth Schumann and Kathleen Ferrier. The clef below his signature he only added after a concert. His photo is a poignant one, with his daughter Gretchen, who in 1939 in Zürich was killed by her estranged husband, who then committed suicide.

After the French composer **Albert Roussel** (1869-1937) signed a year before his death, comes **Adolf Busch** (1891-1952), the brother of the conductor, Fritz Busch, who was the first music director of Glyndebourne Opera. Although he was a sought-after concerto player, Adolf preferred chamber music to solo work and formed for many years a duo with his son-in-law Rudolf Serkin. He also had his own Busch Quartet, and their records and CDs are still available today.

The German tenor **Karl Erb** (1877-1958) who follows was famous as the Evangelist in the *St. Matthew Passion*. He performed in Mahler's *Lied von der Erde* many times under Mengelberg with **Ilona Durigo**, who will appear later.

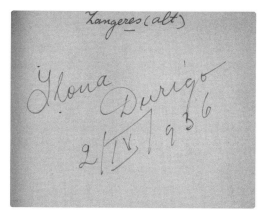

Left: Karl Erb.
Right: Ilona Durigo.

Top and centre left:
Bruno Walter (shown
in the photograph
with his daughter).
Top and centre right:
Albert Roussel.
Bottom: Adolf Busch
(shown in the
photograph with
Rudolf Serkin, piano).

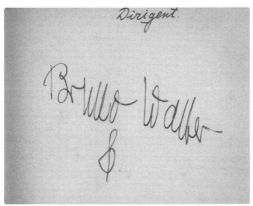

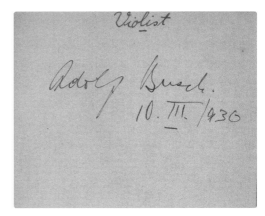

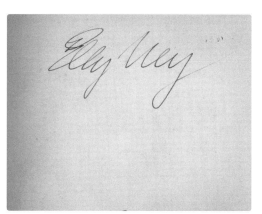

Left: Edwin Fischer.
Right: Elly Ney.

Edwin Fischer (1886-1960), the unassuming Swiss pianist, who lived and worked in Berlin, is the acknowledged mentor, if not teacher of many of this generation's pianists. Alfred Brendel is perhaps the best known of them although he only attended masterclasses. Edwin Fischer was a great classicist and at one time had his own chamber orchestra. Brendel, whose signature does not appear, as he is postwar, is an unusual pianist. After a career of playing the entire repertoire, especially the 'heavy' pieces – *Hammerklavier*, the *Emperor Concerto*, the Brahms concertos – he will now happily conclude a concert with a Haydn sonata, something that Sviatoslav Richter in his later years also did. Brendel also writes a type of short surrealist poetry of a very original and inventive kind, in addition to very readable musical essays. In his younger years he showed considerable painting talent. A latter-day Renaissance man.

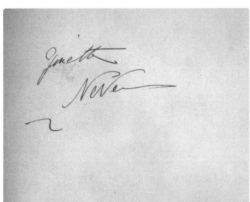

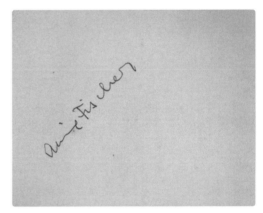

Elly Ney (1882-1968) was the most powerful German lady pianist I ever heard. When playing a Brahms concerto, she was literally able to shake the piano, but like Gieseking, she was a master of the complete repertoire. Unfortunately she was also an ardent Nazi and Hitler's favourite pianist (something I only learned during the war), which meant the end of her career in 1945.

I am happy to have the autograph of **Ginette Neveu** (1919-1949). The career of this brilliant young French violinist was cut short by her untimely death in a plane crash after the war, together with her brother for whom I had turned pages. The plane which crashed in the Azores off Spain also carried the French/Spanish middleweight world-champion boxer, Marcel Cerdan, a long time lover of Edith Piaf. Before boarding their flight a press photo was taken of Ginette Neveu and Marcel Cerdan which, in spite of trying vigorously, I was unable to obtain. A few years later Jacques Thibaud, who had been her teacher, likewise died in a plane crash. Both carried their Stradivariuses to their deaths. When I asked for her autograph, she didn't seem much older than myself.

The following signature belongs to **Yvonne Lefébure** (1898-1986). She had the distinction of being a pupil of both Marguérite Long and Alfred Cortot.

Annie Fischer (1914-1995) was Hungarian, and one of the most complex and probing pianists of her time. Her repertoire was centred on the great Viennese classics, Mozart, Beethoven, Schubert, but it is interesting to learn that in 1933, when she was the youngest of a hundred competitors, she won first prize at the Franz Liszt International Piano Competition in Budapest with her performance of the B Minor Sonata, a work she continued to play until the end of her life.

Dame Myra Hess (1890-1965) was a favourite soloist of Toscanini and made several recordings with him. During World War II, she refused to leave London and gave numerous concerts during the Battle of Britain which she always closed with Bach's chorale *Jesu, Joy of Man's Desiring* as a prayer for survival, as it were. She did that also at her first concert in Amsterdam in 1945, which I heard. It was very moving as a thanksgiving for victory and peace. Another pianist who adopted this chorale as his musical signature throughout his concert career was Dinu Lipatti, beginning in 1935 on the occasion of the death of his composition teacher, Paul Dukas, in Paris.

Moriz Rosenthal (1862-1946) gave me a rather decorative autograph. Rosenthal was one of the oldest living Liszt pupils and he usually played a 19th-century programme - a Liszt piano concerto with orchestra before the intermission, solos afterwards. His technique was fabulous, but he took all the liberties Liszt had taught him, which were a bit old-fashioned by the time I heard him. In his time he was famous for his barnstorming arrangements of Strauss waltzes!

Carl Schuricht (1880-1967) and **Ignaz Neumark** regularly conducted the Residentie Orchestra (in the Hague) during its summer season in Scheveningen.

Sara Scuderi is remembered today only by a few cognoscenti, but she was Puccini's favourite Tosca, and I heard her in Amsterdam with a touring Italian opera troupe. She

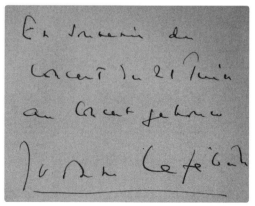

Left: Sara Scuderi.
Right: Yvonne Lefébure

Top and centre
left:Dame Myra Hess.
Top and centre right:
Moriz Rosenthal.
Bottom left: Carl
Schuricht.
Bottom right:Ignaz
Neumark

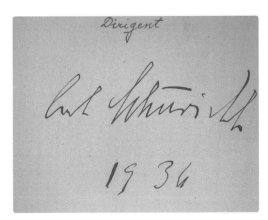

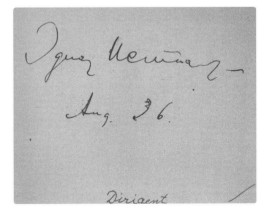

Other Musicians at the Concertgebouw

spent her last years in Casa Verdi in Milan (or Villa di Riposo, as it is properly called), the home that Verdi built for retired singers, and which he said was his greatest achievement in life. In 1984, a well-known Swiss cineast, Daniel Schmid, who came from the same village where we now live, made a film of Villa di Riposo and its inhabitants, which he charmingly called 'Il Bacio di Tosca' – 'The Kiss of Tosca'. He persuaded some of the retired singers, who were in their eighties, to sing in the film, including Scuderi, who still produced a beautiful and romantic sound.

The next musician is **Andrés Segovia** (1893-1987), the Spanish classical guitarist, who filled the large hall of the Concertgebouw without any difficulty.

The violinist **Guila Bustabo** (1919-2002), who started her career as a child prodigy, was in her twenties by the time she gave me her autograph. She lived to a ripe old age, but even then maintained the appearances of a child, wearing her hair long and cut in front in a fringe. She was a very talented violinist.

The following autograph is of **Václav Talich** (1883-1961), the conductor of the Czech Philharmonic Orchestra. He was in Amsterdam with the Prague National Opera for a performance of *The Bartered Bride* of Smetana, Prodaná Nev_stá, which he called a 'symphony of joy'. He was one of the most talented conductors of pre and postwar Europe.

Andrés Segovia.

Top and centre left:
Guila Bustabo.
Bottom left: Vaclav
Talich.
Right: David Oistrakh

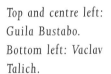

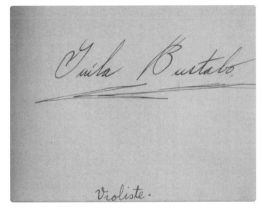

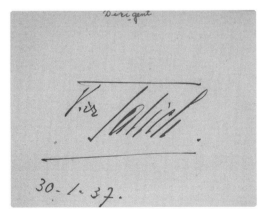

David Oistrakh (1908-1974), the famous Russian violinist, won the Reine Elizabeth Concours in Brussels in 1937, while I happened to be there on holiday. He participated by special dispensation, in spite of his age, because it was realized he was prohibited to leave Russia previously. At that time the competition was still called the Ysaÿe Concours, after the Queen's teacher. It was almost his first exposure to the West, and when I asked for his signature he wrote in cyrillic script. After the war he conquered the world and died too young in Amsterdam in 1974. Some thirty years later I heard him in a recital with Svatoslav Richter, when they played the César Frank Sonata. In Richter's own words: "Oistrakh played it well, of course, but didn't take it seriously, considering it little better than salon music, whereas I was passionate about this wonderful work. After all, isn't it Vinteuil's Sonata in Proust?"

The following autograph and musical motif was written by a man who is now completely forgotten: **Josef Jongen**, then Director of the Brussels Conservatory. At the same time I heard in Brussels the young French composer **François de Bourguignon**, who signed with an amusing quotation from his *Oiseaux de Nuit* (Birds of the Night). He is followed by **Désiré Défauw** (1885-1960), the Belgian conductor, who went on to become conductor of the Chicago Symphony Orchestra, ten years before Fritz Reiner. We seem to be on a French stretch: **Henri Rabaud** was the Principal Conduc-

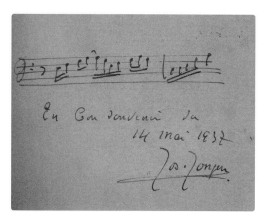

Top left: Josef Jongen.
Top right: Françoise de Bourgignon.
Bottom left: Désir Dáfauw.
Bottom right: Henri Rabaud

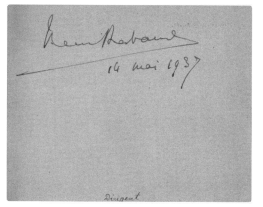

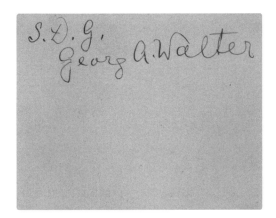

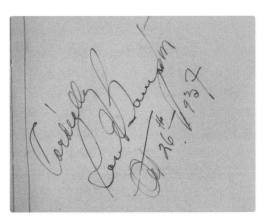

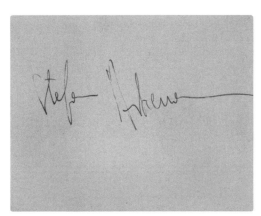

tor of the Paris Opéra, who with the entire cast had come to Amsterdam to conduct Paul Dukas' *Ariane et Barbe-Bleu* for the Dutch Wagner Society, to which I have referred in detail earlier.

Georg A. Walter was a well-known German baritone of his days, whose main claim to fame was as Evangelist in the *St Matthew Passion* and as teacher of Dietrich Fischer-Dieskau. The initials SDG stand for *Soli Deo Gloria*, the words with which Bach prefaced his works.

Stefan Askenase (1896-1985) was a great Polish Chopin player, no relation of today's Vladimir Ashkenazy. What is little known is that after the war he was one of the teachers Martha Argerich was closest to. Argerich, a hugely talented but very complicated personality, fell into her first depression in 1964 at the age of twenty-two. Stefan Askenase and his strong-willed wife helped her to get out of it, and in 1965 at the age of twenty four, she won first prize in the International Chopin Competition in Warsaw, after which she never looked back.

The next autograph is signed 'Cordially, Rose Bampton'. **Rose Bampton** was the acknowledged first lyrical soprano of the Metropolitan Opera of New York. She rarely came to Amsterdam and I was pleased to be able to hear her when I turned pages for her

Top and centre left:
Lener String Quartet
(Jenö Lener is second
from the left).
Below: Paul
Hindemith.

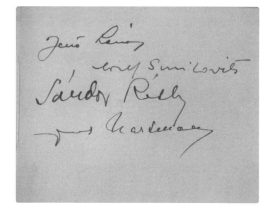

accompanist. She was also a large lady, but she had no problems vigorously cliombing and descending the stairs to the platform.

The previous page contains four autographs, of the **Léner String Quartet**, one of the best known string quartets of its day, named after its primarius, Jénö Léner.

I am proud to have the autograph of **Paul Hindemith** (1895-1963), one of the most important composers of this century, who, as mentioned earlier, had to leave Germany in 1937 because Goebbels considered his music to be degenerate. He was also an excellent viola player, and I remember that on the night that I asked him for his autograph he played his own concerto, *Der Schwanendreher* (Swan turner) with the Concertgebouw Orchestra under Mengelberg.

On the next page we start with the Italian composer **Alfredo Casella**. He wrote one of his own motifs in my book. An interesting detail is that in the date on which he signed the autograph he added in Roman characters "XVI", which was the 16th year since Mussolini's march on Rome.

Alexander Borowsky, a Polish pianist, now practically forgotten, but in his time a great Bach player. He played the *Goldberg Variations* which was rarely done in his day and *Der Kunst der Fugue* (The Art of the Fugue) in their totality, and by heart, something Andras Schiff and Murray Perahia do today.

Here are the inseparable French composer-pianist and baritone duo, **Francis Poulenc** (1899-1963) and **Pierre Bernac** (1899-1979). They, as many today will remember, represented the best in the art of Lieder singing, from baroque to classic, French, German Romantic and modern, especially Poulenc's own compositions, which remain popular to this day.

Eva Liebenberg is a now forgotten German contralto, but since she gave a dedication to me, I include it here.

The conductor **Oswald Kabasta** (186?-1946) was conductor of one of the best orchestras in Germany before the War, the Bavarian Radio Symphony Orchestra, and a fervent Nazi (of which I was completely unaware). He committed suicide in 1946 together with his wife.

He is followed by **Georg Kulenkampff** (1898-1948), one of the best German violinists of his generation. He also played chamber music and toured widely both before and during the war with Wilhelm Kempff, the pianist. Towards the end of the war Kulenkampff fled to Switzerland. He played there in a trio with Edwin Fischer and Enrico Mainardi, with whom he had already played in the 1930s, and died not long afterwards.

Darius Milhaud (1892-1974), the great French composer, added a motif from his own music to his autograph. Then follows **Egon Wellesz** (1885-1974), who belonged to the Second Viennese School, but was not as well known as Schoenberg, Alban Berg and Webern. He also added his own motif.

Top and centre:
Francis Poulenc and
Pierre Bernac.
Bottom left: Alfredo
Casella.
Bottom right:
Alexander Borovski.

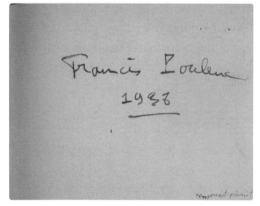

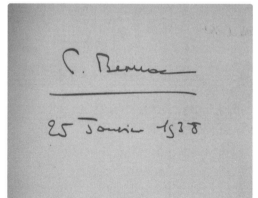

Top left: Eva
Liebenberg.
Top right: Oswald
Kabasta.
Centre left: Georg
Kulenkampff.
Centre right and
below: Darius
Milhaud.

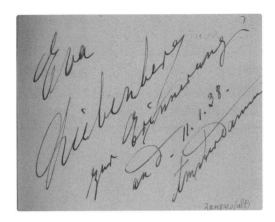

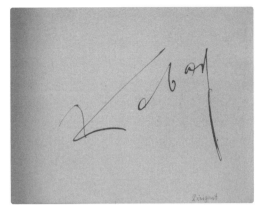

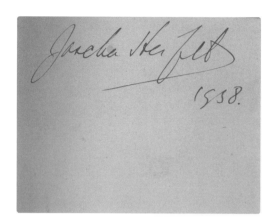

Top: Jascha Heifetz.
Centre left and below:
Kolisch Quartet
(Rudolf Kolisch is on
the left).
Centre right: Egon
Wellesz.

Turning the Pages

Top left: Ernst Křenek.
Right and bottom left:
Zino Francescatti.

Four signatures appear on the opposite page: the **Kolisch Quartet**, another very prominent string ensemble. Rudolf Kolisch was the brother-in-law of Arnold Schoenberg. He lost the use of his left hand in an accident before the war and re-trained himself so that he could finger with his right hand, his left becoming his bowing arm - an astonishing feat. Later in life he wrote a book, *Tempi in Beethoven*, on which he had consulted Schoenberg.

The violinist **Jascha Heifetz** (1901-1987) should not be missing in any autograph book. He came to Holland infrequently but his concerts were always sold out. I turned the pages for him and he mentioned that his unerring intonation was to some degree due to the fact that he used steel strings, and not like most others in his day, gut strings. His uncanny precision at speed was in no small measure due to his rapid bowing technique. It was said that when he appeared on the scene in the 1920s, many violinists developed a 'Heifetz syndrome', a kind of inferiority complex induced by Heifetz's staggering talent and his meteoric rise to fame. Mischa Elman, who was the pre-eminent violinist in the early decades of the last century, appears to have contracted this 'disease'.

Another composer: **Ernst Křenek** (1900-1991). He was a pupil of the Austrian composer Franz Schreker and was close to Schoenberg and his Viennese School. Most of them

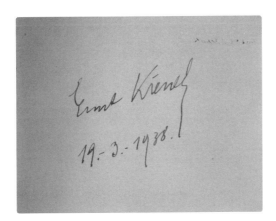

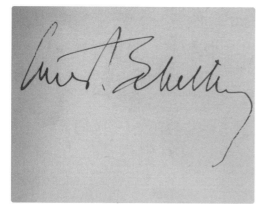

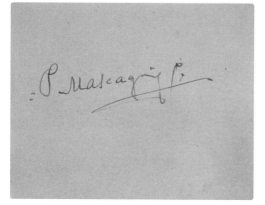

emigrated to America, Křenek among them in 1938, returning to Europe after the war.
He enjoyed a great success with his opera *Johnny spielt auf.*

The French violinist **Zino Francescatti** (1902-1991) was very famous in his day, and
still remembered by many people for his infallible technique and special tone. He gave
me a dedicated autograph with the opening bars of a Beethoven sonata. I turned the
pages for his accompanist. On other occasions he was joined by the pianist Robert
Casadesus with programmes of equal partnership. Their recordings are still available.

Above is **Ernest Schelling**, the composer. The signature that follows is of a man as old
as any of the surviving Liszt pupils in this collection: **Pietro Mascagni** (1863-1945), the
composer of *Cavalleria Rusticana*. He visited Amsterdam to conduct that opera with a visiting opera troupe, and I remember that he was too old to stand up and so was given a
chair from which to conduct.

The opposite page contains the autograph of a Polish pianist, who was a great Chopin
player, **Raoul Koczalski**. He was the subject of an earlier-quoted anecdote Arthur Rubinstein used to tell. We are coming slowly to the end of the second book, and here is
another string quartet, the **Pro Arte Quartet**, of Belgian nationality: Alphonse Onnou,
Laurent Halleux, Germain Prévost and Robert Maas (brother of the pianist Marcel Maas).

Top and centre left:
Pro *Arte* Quartet (left
to right *Alphonse
Onnou, Robert Maas,
Germain Prévost and
Laurent Halleux*).
Centre right: *Raoul
Koczalski*.
Below: *Julius Patzak*.

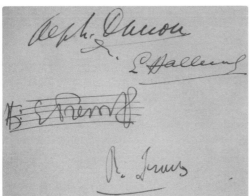

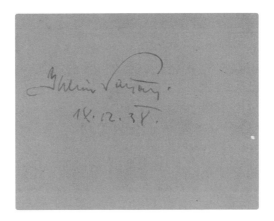

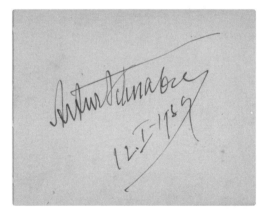

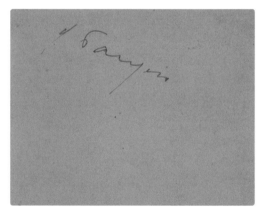

Top and centre left:
Artur Schnabel.
Top and centre right:
Charles Panzera and
his wife.
Bottom left:Jan
Smeterlin.
Bottom right: Ignaz
Friedman.

The first signature in my fourth book of autographs (see p93) is of **Julius Patzak** (1898-1974), the great and enduring Viennese tenor, equally at home in opera, lieder and oratorio. I heard him in *Das Lied von der Erde* under Bruno Walter and after the war in *Fidelio* under Klemperer. Interestingly for a singer, Patzak was a regular smoker all his life.

Another treasured autograph of mine is of **Artur Schnabel** (1882-1951), the pianist who said that he only played music that was better than could be performed. I asked for his autograph after one of his famous Beethoven recitals, with his unforgettable interpretation of the Diabelli Variations. Many of today's pianists consider him their teacher or at least mentor. I also heard him with his son, Karl-Ulrich, playing Mozart's Concerto for Two Pianos.

Next is the hard to decipher autograph of the Swiss baritone **Charles Panzéra** (1896-1976), - the photo shows him with his wife and accompanist Magdaleine Panzéra-Baillot. Panzéra trained and lived in Paris. He is followed by **Jan Smeterlin**, the Polish Chopin player. The pianist **Ignaz Friedman** (1882-1948) was also Polish, and was the piano partner of Bronislaw Huberman, the violinist, who also appears in this book. Below is a nice autograph of **Lola Bobesco**, who signed: *sympathiquement, Lola Bobesco*. She was a very young Romanian violinist who had begun as a prodigy. She took Belgian nationality, and, as far as I know is still living. **Igor Markevitch** (1912-1983), was a friend of Diaghilev, Jean Cocteau and Paul Sacher, who called him the most significant composer of his time. Markevitch went on to become a conductor and the author of very readable musical essays. His fame as a conductor certainly seemed to last longer than that of his compositions. He signed his autograph "1-ère [première - as he wrote it] du *Nouvel Age*", which was his most recent orchestral work, performed in 1939.

The next page starts with **Mario Castelnuovo-Tedesco** (1895-1968), the Italian composer who wrote film music and light classical works and dedicated his autograph to me with a phrase from his *Alt Wien*.

Heinz Tietjen (1881-1967) was the powerful general intendant of all Prussian state theatres and artistic director at Bayreuth from 1927 to 1945. He was in Amsterdam for an opera performance of the Wagner Society by one of his German opera ensembles.

Left: Lola Bobesco.
Right: Igor Markevitch.

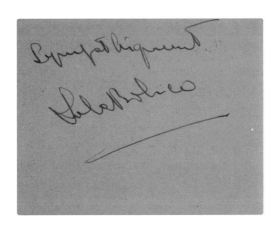
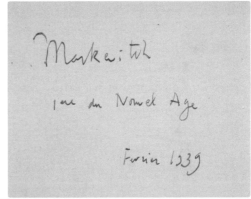

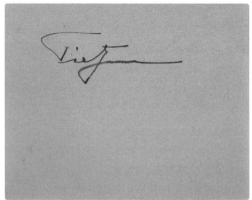

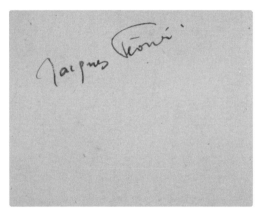

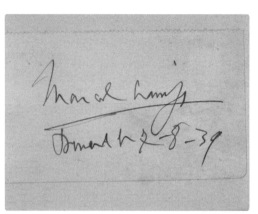

Top left: Mario Castelnuovo-Tedesco.
Top right: Heinz Tietjen.
Bottom left: Jacques Février.
Bottom right: Marcel Ciampi.

The French pianist **Jacques Février** (1900-1979), came out of the school of Alfred Cortot and made a great name for himself. Ravel's Piano Concerto for the Left Hand was dedicated to him after the composer became dissatisfied with the way it was performed by Paul Wittgenstein, the work's original dedicatee.

The next signature is that of **Marcel Ciampi** (1891-1980), whom I mentioned earlier in connection with Hephzibah Menuhin. This autograph was given to me in Dinard, France, where I spent the summer vacation with my parents. **Egon Petri** (1881-1962), the disciple of Busoni who follows, was a famous pianist in his day, whose name seems almost forgotten now. His father was a well-known violinist who was a close friend of Busoni, and Egon became one of his pupils.

Next is **Kerstin Thorborg**, then still young, who later became the famous Wagner soprano at the Metropolitan Opera. I treasure my autograph of **Pierre Monteux** (1875-1964), with a dedication commemorating his concert of 12 October 1939. Monteux often guest conducted in Amsterdam; his photograph appears on p 54 with Stravinsky.

There follows an autograph of the famous and very popular **Jussi Björling** (1911-1960), who died too young, and **Joseph Szigeti** (1892-1973), the tall Hungarian violinist who will never be forgotten. His piano accompanist was the Russian Nikita Maga-

Top left: Egon Petri.
Top right: Kerstin
Thorborg.
Centre left: Pierre
Monteux.
Centre right: Jussi
Björling.
Bottom left: Joseph
Szigeti.
Bottom right: Erna
Sack.

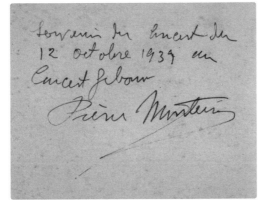

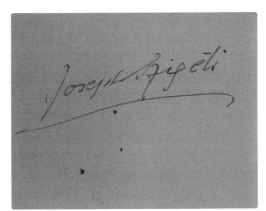

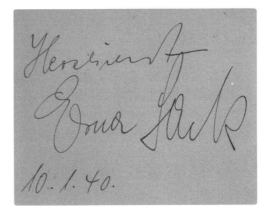

loff, who became his son-in-law. Together with Mischa Elman, he was the premier violinist in pre-Heifetz days. I remember now that he was often the partner in a duo with Ignaz Friedman.

Above is a little curiosity: **Erna Sack** with a dedication: 'herzlichst' (warmly). Erna Sack was a famous German operetta and coloratura soprano. On the next page is the conductor **Paul Paray**, who after the war was a regular conductor of the Israel Philharmonic

Orchestra, but is most closely associated with the Detroit Symphony Orchestra, because of his many recordings with it.

We are coming to the end of my pre-war period and here is the famous **Calvet String Quartet** who signed in February 1940. Shortly thereafter the Quartet broke up when the second violinist went to America, changing his name to Daniel Guilet. He became leader of Toscanini's orchestra and founded not only his own Guilet Quartet, but also the Beaux Arts Trio, still in existence today with Menachem Presler. The Calvet String Quartet briefly re-started after the war with different players.

I do not know how the British conductor **Sir Adrian Boult** (1889-1983) managed to come to Holland but here he is. Another musical motif and dedication come from the cellist **Gaspar Cassadó** (1897-1966). The motif is a chord from Schubert's Arpeggione Sonata. Following him is **Enrico Mainardi** (1897-1976), an equally famous cellist, and

Top and bottom right: Calvet String Quartet (left to right: Joseph Calvet, Daniel Guilevich, Leon Pascal, Paul Mas). Bottom left: Paul Paray.

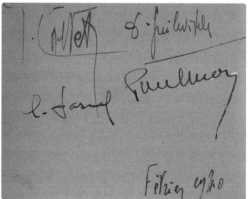

Top and centre left: Sir
Adrian Boult.
Top and centre right:
Gaspar Casadó.
Bottom left: Enrico
Mainardi.
Bottom right:
Hermann Abenroth.

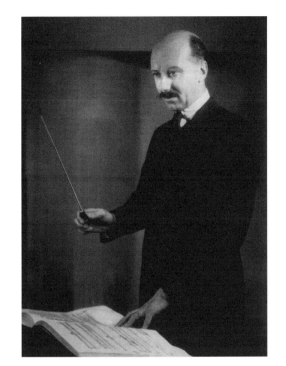

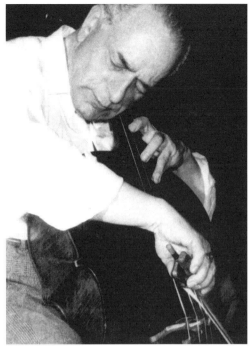

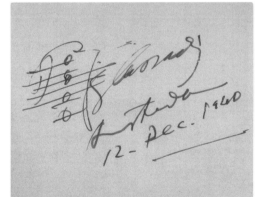

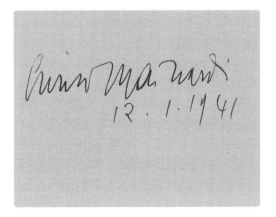

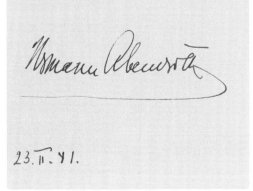

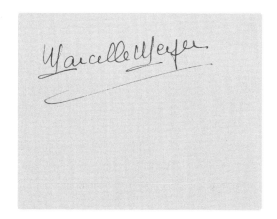

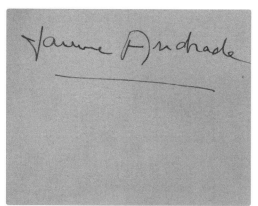

Top left: Marcelle Meyer.

Top right: Janine Andrade.

Centre left and below: Louis Zimmerman.

Centre right: Hubert Bahrwaser.

The photograph below shows, from left to right: Henri van Goudoever, composer and occasional conductor of the Utrecht Orchestra; Louis Zimmerman, concertmaster of the Concergebouw Orchestra and Willem van Otterloo, conductor of the City of Utrecht Orchestra. The dedication reads 'To the highly talented conductor and composer Willem van Otterloo in memory of the 26th September 1934 and of Louis Zimmerman' followed by a solo viiolin motif.

in fact I see this autograph was signed in 1941. Being Italian, of course, he could come to occupied Holland. And here is **Hermann Abendroth**, the German conductor, signing also in February 1941. Finally come the signatures of **Marcelle Meyer** (1897-1958), another pianist of the Cortot school, and **Janine Andrade** (1918-), then a well-known French violinist.

I would like to conclude my autograph collection with a selection of pre-war Dutch artists. **Louis Zimmerman** (1873-1954), whose autograph and photograph are shown opposite, was Concertmaster of the Concertgebouw Orchestra in the 1920s and 1930s. As soloist he chose Beethoven's Violin Concerto so often that people referred to it as 'the violin concerto of Zimmerman'. A recording of it has been issued as a CD in Japan.

In order that readers do not gain the impression that all first desk players of the Concertgebouw Orchestra were foreigners, I will mention a few of the Dutch solo players. They include my friend **Haakon Stotijn**, the fabulous solo oboist, and probably the single most valuable player, of whom I have already spoken in the first part of this book, and the first bassoon **Tom de Klerk**. These two, with the solo flautist **Hubert Bahrwaser** (1906-1985) were also members of the Concertgebouw Quintet (below). Though German by birth, Bahrwaser was resident in Holland. Also on the first desk were the outstanding trumpettist Marinus Komst, the tympanist with the good Dutch name of

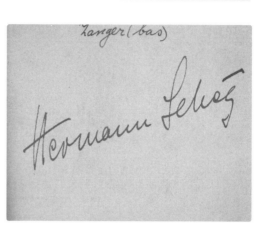

Left and top right:
Carel van Leeuwen
Boomkamp.
Below right: Herman
Schey.

Smit, the solo cellist Henk van Wezel and the first double bass Hendrik Stips, who for many years represented the orchestra in negotiations with the management.

Carel van Leeuwen Boomkamp (1906-2000) was Holland's best known viola da gamba player, and only recently passed away. He was the cellist of the Netherlands String Quartet after the war. During the war he played sonatas at chamber music evenings with Eduard van Beinum, and trios with van Beinum's wife Sepha taking the violin part. Next to his autograoh is that of **Herman Schey** (1895-1981), a bass-baritone, who had emigrated from Germany.

The pianist and composer **Henriette Bosmans** (1895-1952) was in her early thirties when she gave me her autograph. She came from a musical family. Her father was at one time principal cellist of the Concertgebouw Orchestra, her mother a concert pianist. From the latter she inherited her pianistic talents, although composition became her main métier. I asked for her autograph after a Sunday matinée concert, when she played her own *Concertino for Piano* under Mengelberg. Fortunately, this charming Ravel-inspired work has not been forgotten, and is part of the repertoire of, among others, the Dutch pianist Ronald Brautigam. The pianist **Willem Andriessen** (1887-1964)similarly came

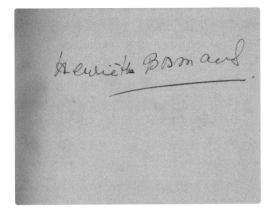
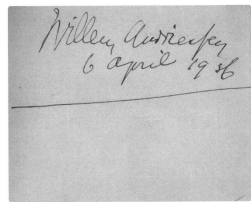
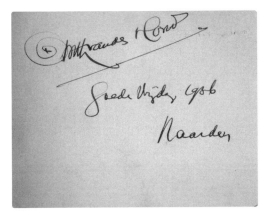
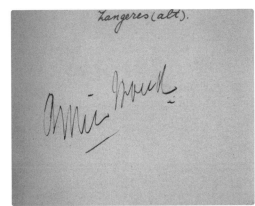

Top left: Henriette Bosmans.
Top right: Willem Andriessen.
Bottom left: Anthon van der Horst.
Bottom right: Annie Woud.

from a family of composers and performing musicians still active today. He was also Director of the Amsterdam Conservatoire.

Anthon van der Horst (1899-1965) was an organist and conducted the earliest Dutch unabridged performance of Bach's St. Matthew Passion in the church of Naarden. Next to his autograph is that of the contralto **Annie Woud** (1901-?), known for her Passion performances.

Rosa Spier (1891-1967), whose autograph appears on the next page, was the harpist of the Concertgebouw Orchestra. After the war she took up an invitation to found a home for retired artists, which was then named after her. It is still going under the name 'Rosas Spier House' at Laren, Wirlk Holland, and among its residents are a number of retired members of the Concertgebouw Orchestra.

Also on the next page is the autograph of **Jaap Stotijn** (1891-1970) who was first oboeist of the Residentie Orchestra of The Hague. His son Haakon became first oboe in the Concertgebouw. Haakon was a good friend, which is perhaps the reason I never asked for his autograph. Jaap and Haakon were among the first oboeists to introduce the vibrato tone (another was the English performer Leon Goossens), thereby modernizing the old nasal French style, which Haakon's predecessor Blan-

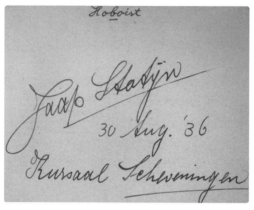

chard employed. I have a wonderful memory of hearing father and son as soloists in a concerto for two oboes specially written for them by Alexander Voormolen. There still exists a recording of it, with Mengelberg conducting the Concertgebouw Orchestra on the TAHRA label.

The soprano **To van der Sluijs** (1902-?), alto **Suze Luger** (1889-1971), tenor **Louis van Tulder** (1892-1969) and bass-baritone **Willem Ravelli** (1892-1980) all appear

Top left: To van der
Sluijs.
Top right: Louis van
Tulder.
Bottom left: Suze Luger.
Bottom right: Willem
Ravelli.

together as they formed for many years the vocal quartet in Beethoven's 9th Symphony, conducted year after year by Mengelberg in his annual Beethoven Cycle..

The violinist **Jan Damen** (1898-1957) was Dutch, born in Breda and trained initially in the Hague. He was really called Damen but used the spelling Dahmen during his tenure as concertmaster in Germany, first in Berlin and then in Dresden. He may have also used that spelling in Sweden, where he was concertmaster in Gothenburg, but by the time he returned to Holland he had reverted to Damen. A German habit remains: he signed himself as 'Professor'. In quoting the opening bars of Beethoven's Violin Concerto he forgot the two sharps behind the clefs. He was no doubt an eminent concertmaster, in which capacity he served the Concertgebouw Orchestra for a few years after the war, when he became a great friend of Eduard van Beinum. He died prematurely in 1957, two years before van Beinum.

The next three autographs belong to composers. On the opposite page is the autograph of **Johan Wagenaar** (1862-1941) who was the best-known pre-war Dutch composer, and whose music is occasionally performed today (his daughter Nelly was a well-known concert pianist). On the next page is the composer **Sem Dresden** (1881-1957) who later became Director of The Hague Conservatory. I do not know whether his music is still

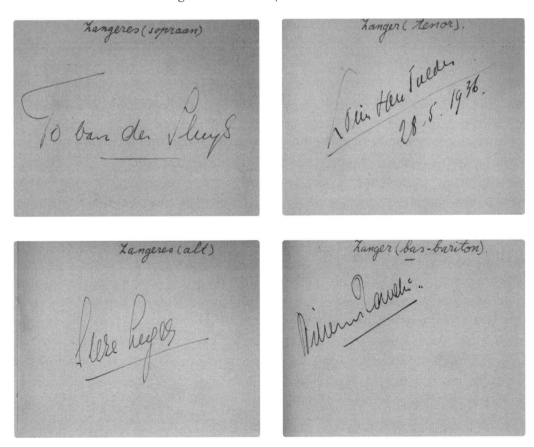

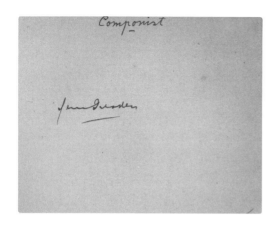

Left: Sem Dresden.
Top left: Peter van
Anrooy.
Centre right: Willem
van Otterloo (see
photo on p 100).
Bottom right: Eduard
Flipse.

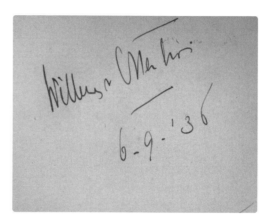

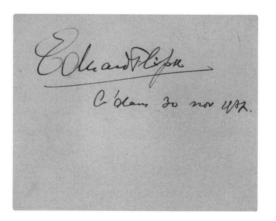

performed. **Peter van Anrooy** (1879-1954) was both composer and conductor. Sadly his reputation did not survive the war.

    Willem van Otterloo (1907-1978), whose photograph appears on p 100, was the unforgettable conductor of the Residentie Orchestra in The Hague. In the 1960s, his son Chris became a good friend. Chris was a gifted etcher who lived in Kyoto, where I visit-

Top left and below:
Géza Frid with Zoltan
Kodaly.
Right: Coenraad V.
Bos.

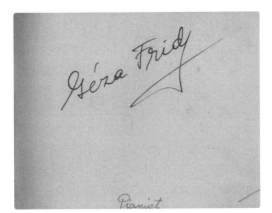

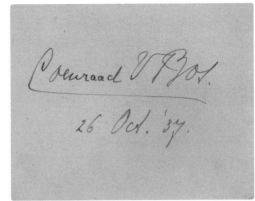

ed him from time to time. His father conducted regularly in Japan, and so I was occasionally invited for lunch by father and son. Willem was a much sought-after conductor in Japan. Another conductor, **Eduard Flipse** (1896-1973) is still remembered for his time with the Rotterdam Philharmonic Orchestra, and as the older brother of the pianist Marinus Flipse. Both brothers appear in the photograph on p70.

Coenraad V. Bos (1875-1955) was a Dutch pianist who lived in New York, where he built up a considerable reputation as an accompanist. I remember him as small, bald, and lively, with very small hands. I turned pages for him when he accompanied a number of American artists. Another pianist, **Gézà Frid** (1904-1989) I have counted as an honorary

Dutchman since, though he was Hungarian by birth and kept up his contact with Hungary, he settled in Amsterdam. His percussive style was particularly suited for Bartók, whom he usually joined when the latter visited Holland.

My last Dutch autograph also comes under the category of 'honorary'. **Gérard Hekking** (1879-1942) was the French member of the Hekking cellist clan, an essentially Dutch family which produced numerous cellists, notably Anton and André.

Many of these pre-war Dutch artists were little-known overseas. It was not because they were inferior, but because artist managements active on the foreign circuit preferred international stars to local celebrities.

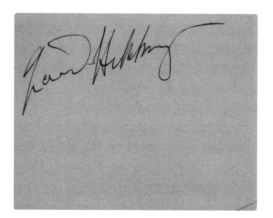

Gérard Hekking.

3

Reminiscences of the Concertgebouw 1934-1940

With the Amsterdam Concertgebouw taking such a prominent place in my memories, a word about its halls and their ambience seems to be in order. The large hall, seating 1600, has outstanding accoustic qualities which are comparable to other halls built in the same period (late 19th century) such as the Musikverein in Vienna and the Tonhalle in Zürich. It is also well-proportioned, warm and welcoming. The orchestra sits on all sides, surrounded by the audience, who in recitals can sit quite close to the artists. For a large hall it has an unusual atmosphere of intimacy. There are no segregated boxes, cheap seats or standing room only. Everyone pays the same price and feels part of one audience.

The soloists' room (as it was called) for the large hall is situated on the balcony floor. In the 1930s it was used by conductors as well as soloists, and the concertmaster of the orchestra was also allowed in. At that time it was furnished and decorated entirely in red plush, in the style of 1900. The way from the soloist's room to the platform was – as I have mentioned elsewhere – a bit inconvenient. One had to go along the balcony corridor for about fifty feet and enter on the opposite side through or next to the 'Chairman's Box'. This was the only Box in the house and reserved for Directors, Impresarios and a few others who were allowed to enter and leave unseen during performances. The Box looked down on the platform and had a low gate leading to it. To reach the concert area one had to descend some twenty steps. These steps were inconvenient, too wide for one step and too narrow for two. A number of lady performers simply refused to negotiate them and had a screen set up for them in front of the organ, which only required two or three steps to reach.

The recital hall, oval in shape, with a capacity of 400, also had excellent accoustics and, of course, a more natural intimacy. This small hall had in those days a so-called tuning room next to it, where the orchestra would assemble. There was a small room inside it which provided recitalists with a degree of privacy. It was fairly austere.

This was the hall where before the war a regular audience came by subscription to hear Mozart and Beethoven by 'their own' Lili Kraus and Simon Goldberg, forming a bond of shared feelings that was almost palpable in the audience and on the platform. Here there was no question of whether the sparks would fly; it was there from the start, ready in anticipation. I remember a concert where at the end the public, totally spontaneously, rose to its feet in homage to the young performers. Lili Kraus stood facing the audience and saw in the first row, in her usual place, a very old lady, Mrs de Vries, who never missed a concert and always came backstage. Lili Kraus took the few steps down off the platform, went over to Mrs De Vries and embraced her. In doing so she embraced the entire audience. It seemed totally natural to everyone. Lili came back to the piano with tears in her eyes. They then played the simplest of encores: the short Schubert Sonatine, the first piece on every amateur's repertoire. It was very moving.

Recitals were usually programmed with the 'heavy' works performed before the intermission (it is interesting to note that in operas the climax also often comes at the end of the second act, as in *The Marriage of Figaro* or *Falstaff*). After the intermission came lighter pieces and some fireworks, to leave plenty of room for encores. Then the audience was on its feet and crowded forward in front of the platform, where they would remain, in front of and just below the artists.

Amsterdam audiences were always slow to warm up – as were some soloists - but once the rapport had been established, it was quickly felt on the platform and the bond was never lost. A reciprocal reaction set in. Performers always asked themselves in private and in public why Amsterdam audiences were so special and so loyal. I think - and here I venture a purely personal opinion - that it might have had something to do with the composition of the audience and the time in which we lived. Amsterdam always had a fairly large Jewish population, perhaps fifteen per cent or more, a bit like Berlin. As in Berlin, the Jewish intelligentsia and bourgeoisie were highly assimilated and felt first Dutch and then Jewish. But Amsterdam also had a large number of very poor Jews, who lived from hand to mouth and depended often on familial or community support, which was always forthcoming. The Jews were aware of this chasm in their community. Contrary to Germany, Austria, France and even Italy, there was no trace of anti-semitism in Holland, quite the contrary, and in time of war, a sense of solidarity.

In the second half of the thirties, an oppressed Jewish group arrived in Amsterdam. These were exiled Jews from Germany, mostly upper middle class, who had often been able to bring some of their money, if not other assets. They were well-educated and cultured and soon found their way to the Concertgebouw. Here they heard their own exiled fellow Jewish artists, which created a special bond. Altogether there was undoubtedly a fairly large proportion of Jewish members (both Dutch and immigrant) in any Concertgebouw audience and they were often, but inconspicuously, the flame that started the fire of enthusiasm, which was born of a yearning for shared feelings. Thanks to the Concertgebouw Orchestra and Mengelberg, Amsterdam had a musically well-educated audience of considerable sophistication. There was, for example, no audience in the world in the first half of the century which knew Mahler better than Amsterdam (after Hitler came to power, of course, Mahler could no longer be played in Germany). This, combined with the feeling of solidarity with regularly returning Jewish artists, may be one explanation - there may be others - of the warmth and loyalty of Amsterdam audiences. It is no exaggeration to say that a large proportion of the performing artists were Jews who had been denied their traditional platform in Germany and Austria, but were warmly and undiscriminately welcomed in Amsterdam. They included Walter, Klemperer, Kleiber, Heifetz, Horowitz, Rubinstein, Hess, Feuermann, Kraus, Goldberg, Milstein; the list can be continued ad libidum. This particular audience mix, of course, vanished after the war, to be replaced, I am told, by a no less warm and responsive public today.

Looking back, I have devoted the greater part of this book to famous protagonists, and for obvious reasons. In the course of my 'work' as page-turner, however, I also came fairly close to the 'ordinary' people who make a concert hall tick, and for whom the Concertgebouw was simply a workplace. They ranged from porters to ushers, carpenters and handymen. Sometimes I needed their assistance when another piano stool or music stand or simply coffee, tea, hot or not so hot water was unexpectedly but instantantaneously required. Artists or impresarios simply passed these requests on to me and I had to find the right person backstage to carry out the order. I am happy to say that I never met with an uncooperative or sullen response. Young as I was (really a schoolboy), they always saw me as another worker who had a job to do and therefore had to be treated like a fellow worker.

The people at the Concertgebouw I came to know best were the porters at the artists' entrance, who saw me appear regularly in all kinds of weather on my bicycle. I remember two in particular: Visser and Rosenbrand. Middle-aged and Amsterdam-born and bred, they both spent their entire working lives in the same job. They invariably invited me into their little cubicle - and little it was, with just enough room for a table and chair and a small cabinet for a thermos flask of coffee and some cups. I became especially friendly with Visser (Mr. Visser to me, of course), whose entire life story I came to hear over the course of many years. Those were the depression years, and life was hard for simple wage-earners with large families to feed. His monologues mostly ended with ever-present money problems. The porters always invited me to share their coffee, which was often 'ersatz', and I never saw any of them taking hard liquor on the job, even on bitterly cold nights. I tried to reciprocate their kindness with small services: often people would leave messages for arriving artists, and I would hand them over or convey them in the appropriate language. Sometimes there were briefcases, parcels and even suitcases that had to be transported to the artists' room, four flights up, with no lift, and I would take care of these odd jobs since the doormen were not allowed to leave their posts. They in turn would reciprocate by allowing me to nip upstairs if an artist had somehow managed to escape me on arrival. I even remember discovering late one night after a concert at which I had to 'work' that my bicycle had a flat tyre. Visser allowed me to use a bicycle a member of the orchestra had left in his care in the parking area. Some, not all, of the ushers were also kind to me. Occasionally an impresario would let me in to a concert which was sold out, even in the so-called Blue Hall behind the balcony. A friendly usher would show me to a seat reserved for a fireman, which was something that was completely against regulations. I have never forgotten those faithful friends, because that is what they became. Another person I will not forget is Joelen, the ever-present piano tuner, a true jewel of his profession, and always instantly able to solve the most complicated problems.

Returning to a more elevated level, a few words are in order about that much vilified species, the impresario, immortalized over two centuries ago by Mozart's *Schauspieldirektor*. There were several impresarios working in pre-war Holland, specifically Amsterdam, and I have selected two at opposite ends of the spectrum. The most important impresario was a man with the deceptively Dutch name of De Koos, who was in fact Hungarian. He was among the wave of Hungarian immigrants who found refuge in Holland between the World Wars. He was a large and imposing figure of a man, who never lost his native accent, which somehow seemed in keeping with the public image of the impresario (a bit like the Hungarian 'Count' in *My Fair Lady*). His past had given him a wealth of connections and he was no doubt able to bring many renowned artists to the Concertgebouw. He never bothered much about other venues. Another aspect of his past was that he had personally experienced financial ruin and was henceforth mainly concerned with avoiding a repetition of that fate. His was not exactly a pleasant personality, but his competence earned him respect. I often 'worked' for him (he was in fact, as mentioned earlier, the initiator of my page turning career after my début with Lili Krauss), but we never developed a personal relationship.

At the other extreme was a non-profit organisation with the cosy name of 'Art Circle for Everyone' (Kunstkring Voor Allen). This was a kind of cooperative society which was fairly primitively organized, and on occasion not organized at all. Its committee members hardly spoke any foreign languages, but its purpose in life was to make concerts accessible to every purse. Because it was not a professional impressariat, artists were contractually free to perform under its auspices. Many did so with alacrity and often at reduced fees. The results were very low-priced tickets and an impressive roster of artists, which included Milstein, Brailowsky, Bartók, Menuhin, and many others who came back year after year.

I regularly turned pages for the society and often acted as interpreter and general go-between. The president, whose name deserves mention here, Mr. van Ruyven, was an unassuming man of impeccable musical taste, but little knowledge of languages, and he usually rang me himself when my services were required. He was always ready to give me a free ticket to other concerts. I do not think anyone has ever written the history of this worthwhile society which was not revived after the war.

Reasonable as the Kunstkring's tickets were, they could not match the price of the Concertgebouw's own 'Popular Concerts' ('Volksconcerten'). If I remember correctly, their price was FLS 0.78 (USD 0.34 in today's money), and this included FLS 0.16 'amusement tax' ('Vermakelijkheidsbelasting')! These concerts were usually conducted by Eduard van Beinum, who thereby permanently endeared himself with the Amsterdam public.

An important part of a city's musical life are its music critics, the best of whom form public opinions and taste. There were many different critics working in Amsterdam before the war, but since they reflect different aspects of the city's concert life, each deserves a place in this story. The Nestor of Amsterdam's music critics was **Herman Rutters** (1879-1961), who wrote for Het Handelsblad. He was an erudite man, who also taught at the Conservatory. He maintained (probably deliberately) a remarkably slovenly appearance, which surprised many who knew his immaculate writing style. He was more of a musicologist than a critic and often devoted three-quarters of his column to a historical and musicological exposé of a work, which would have suited many readers better if it had come before rather than after the concert. Comments on the performers came as a sort of afterthought. In Holland, at least, he was the first to coin the phrase 'cathedrals' for Bruckner's symphonies.

L. M. G. Arntzenius (1880-1967) was the vitriolic music critic of De Telegraaf. He was the opposite of Rutters, also in appearance, being always neatly dressed and groomed from head to toe. He was married to a well-known dancer, Yvonne Georgi, who was the leading ballerina of a ballet company that bore her name. They were both forceful characters, and if (as I liked to think) he had had a quarrel with his wife and came to a concert in a foul mood, he was capable of devoting an entire column to the red dress of the singer without saying a word about the music performed. This was perhaps amusing for the readers at breakfast the following day, but unfortunate for the poor artist. One of his expressions that has stuck in my mind was how he invariably referred to the harpsichord as a 'barrel of nails' (Kist met spijkers). He was not alone in his distaste for the instrument. For years writers complained about its 'knitting needle noises' and Sir Thomas Beecham famously drew a more colourful comparison with skeletons, which he probably felt should remain in their cupboards. No one knew Arntzenius' first name; I suspect not even his wife did. He was always L.M.G. An interesting footnote is that in 1931, when the Concertgebouw Orchestra was looking for a second conductor, Arntzenius applied for the position. Monteux chose van Beinum instead.

Mathijs Vermeulen (1888-967) was a gifted composer, married to the daughter of the composer Alphons Diepenbrock, whose name is immortalized in one of the ovals on the balcony of the Concertgebouw. He did not contribute to the daily press, but produced very readable articles in a popular weekly called *De Groene Amsterdammer* ('The Green Amsterdammer'). Vermeulen was possessed of an exquisite bad taste – though not ill-will – which he displayed in public during a Subscription Concert in 1918, at a performance of the Seventh Symphony of Cornelius Dopper (who was also second conductor of the orchestra, long before van Beinum). Vermeulen stood up and shouted "Three cheers for Souza!" (the famous American composer of marches), intended as an outcry against the one-sided, predominantly German-orientated programming at the Concertgebouw. For his trouble Vermeulen was banned from the Concertgebouw for a period of time. In 1920, on the occasion of the great Mahler Festival in Amsterdam, when Mengelberg was fêted by all Dutch and foreign composers, Vermeulen ensured his voice was heard again. He wrote in a review that Mengelberg and his rich friends (meaning the members of the Board of the Concertgebouw) were indirectly responsible for Mahler's death. Instead of having been forced to go to New York, where he intensely disliked the orchestra's mentality, Vermeulen believed that Mahler could have been invited to Amsterdam by Mengelberg and the Board, and given a small stipendium to compose and conduct. His life might thus have been saved or at least prolonged. Vermeulen was referring here to a remark made by Mahler in a letter to Mengelberg written after his first visit to Amsterdam in 1903. He wrote that he had found a "new Heimat in Holland", a statement he repeated on subsequent visits. Interestingly there exists a dedication to Mengelberg's home in Mahler's own hand which reads:

Ich lob' mir Hotel Mengelberg	I praise the Hotel Mengelberg
das sicher ist der Engel Werk	it surely is the work of angels,
damit ein armer Musikant	by helping poor musicians
findt' manches Mal der Heimat Land	sometimes find their homeland

The rhyming pun on Mengelberg's name in the second line is, of course, sadly untranslateable. The musical quotation in Mahler's dedication is from "Das himmliche Leben". Vermeulen's inappropriate remarks caused general indignation - Alma Mahler was in Amsterdam throughout the Festival – and the following year Vermeulen left Holland for France. He returned after the war in 1946 to become music critic again for the *Groene Amsterdamer*. From 1950 he devoted himself exclusively to composing. Van Beinum thought highly of him.

The most interesting and occasionally controversial critic was perhaps the best-known composer of his day, **Willem Pijper** (1894-1947), who wrote for *Het Utrechts Dagblad* (Utrecht Daily News). You will still find a street named after him in many Dutch

Left: *Willem Pijper*.
Right: *Elly Bysterus
Heemskerk (see
following page)*.

cities; my brother in fact lives in one. Pijper was more an essayist than a critic, and I still derive pleasure from re-reading his collected essays in *De Stemvork* ('The Tuning Fork') and *De Kwintencirkel* ('The Circle of Fifths'). The most expert and humane critic was **Paul Sanders** (1891-1967) of *Het Volk* (The People). He emigrated in good time to America, where he made a name for himself as a writer. After the war he returned to Holland as music critic for *Het Parool*. Perhaps passing mention should be made here of a colourful character called **Max Tak**, who was the substitute music critic of *De Telegraaf*. Max Tak was a well-known figure in Amsterdam as leader of the amusement orchestra of the largest and most popular Amsterdam cinema, Tuschinski. In that capacity he arranged music for his orchestra, but at the same time took lessons in classical composition from the Dutch composer Cornelis Dopper, and wrote some music in a serious vein. I remember a *Concertante for Five Violins*. At one time, I believe, he had played violin in the orchestra. He walked around the corridors of the Concertgebouw with a pomposity that somehow suited him. Few people took his concert reviews too seriously, at least I hope the performers did not, but the articles themselves were readable enough. He also emigrated to America.

Before closing I would like to tell a short story about a special lady I mentioned in the earlier chapter on Mengelberg: **Elly Bysterus Heemskerk** (1889-1987). She was a violinist, and a member of the Concertgebouw Orchestra from 1914 to 1951. She was born in Shanghai, where her father was a banker, but the family moved to Hong Kong two years later and there Elly went to school until the age of thirteen. Her fascination with music began in 1898, on the occasion of the coronation of Queen Wilhelmina, when her parents took her to a party on a boat where a group of musicians entertained the guests. Elly stood in front of the violinist in complete awe, and afterwards accepted with alacrity her father's gift of a half-size violin. Once she started playing, she never stopped.

A few years later her father was transferred to Hamburg, where she continued her violin lessons. Her father died young and her mother did something unusual for those days: she took her daughter travelling – to England, France and, of course, to Italy. At the age of nineteen, Elly and her mother settled down in Amsterdam, where she received lessons from a member of the Concertgebouw Orchestra, who was at the same time a teacher at the Conservatory (Director: Daniel de Lange). At the age of twenty three Elly passed her final exams. A friend of hers was already playing in the orchestra (she later married the concertmaster), and Elly was jealous of her. Her chance came sooner than expected: an influenza epidemic felled a number of players and Elly was asked to step in, after auditioning, of course. In 1912 she volunteered to go without pay with the orchestra to Frankfurt to play under Mengelberg, who shortly afterwards asked her to join as a permanent member.

Elly was a young woman who had seen the world, and she had formed her own opinions, which she expressed freely. Mengelberg did not usually appreciate, let alone encourage this, but Elly got away with it, and she soon became a member of his inner circle, and remained so until his death in 1951. Whenever Mengelberg composed something for a friend's birthday, Elly would be among those who would play it. Around this time, 1912, Mengelberg built his chalet in Switzerland, named 'Chasa Mengelberg', and soon Elly started to play hostess to his many visitors during the summer vacations.

When later reminiscing about her years in the orchestra, she would say that she was most impressed by Otto Klemperer in concert ("he conducted with his eyes"), and by Férèncs Fricsay in rehearsal. She also recalled the sharp hearing of Monteux, who was incidentally the only conductor Mengelberg tolerated and even encouraged before 'his'orchestra - provided of course, that he did not play Mahler, which was strictly his personal domain.

Readers may remember that my first glimpse of the orchestra was in 1934, when Carl Muck conducted. Elly, of course, played in the orchestra at this time. Muck was a stiff and somewhat solemn figure, who was never excited, but sometimes sarcastic. She remembered an occasion after a concert when Mengelberg had collapsed in a chair, exhausted. Muck entered, and when he saw Mengelberg said: "Wer schwitzt kann's nicht" (the person who sweats is no good). He touched with his finger the collar of Mengelberg's dress shirt, which had also collapsed, and whispered under his breath "dilettante." Everyone in the room apparently turned rigid in anticipation of an outburst of anger from Mengelberg. A few seconds later there was indeed an outburst from Mengelberg – but of laughter, in which he was joined by Muck. Elly said this was the only time she ever heard Muck laugh. "He was always such a distinguished and courteous person," she said.

Jumping ahead to the 1970s, when Elly was well into her eighties and had become Aunt Elly to everyone, she decided to pay a nostalgic visit to Hong Kong, and my wife and I had the pleasure of receiving her. Because of her advanced age, friends had persuaded her to take a young niece along as companion. I remember well Aunt Elly saying to me on arrival, after the very long flight, "Please look after my niece. She is not feeling well after the long journey." Travelling up the Hong Kong Peak, she recalled how in her young days she had made the trip by rickshaw. She had a wonderful time in Hong Kong, meeting many people who were sometimes two generations younger than herself. She was now an old lady, tall and slim, who always kept hersefl very erect. With her regular features and full head of white hair, she radiated an air of nobility which she certainly possessed.

I kept in touch with Aunt Elly, and one day, a few years after her Hong Kong visit, she invited me to spend a week at Chasa Mengelberg, which had become by then a convalescent home for members of the orchestra. In spite of her age, Aunt Elly managed the household, with the help of some of the ladies. On a later visit to Amsterdam, she mentioned that her housekeeper and companion, a lady also in her eighties, had just passed away. Elly thought this was not quite proper. "Imagine, before me!" she said indignantly. After my visit I was to have lunch with Theo Olof at De Keijzer, a well-known restaurant opposite the Concertgebouw. Aunt Elly suddenly appeared, waving my sunglasses. "You forgot these, so I decided to bring them to you before you realised you had left them behind," she said. She had come all the way by bicycle.

One of my last contacts with Elly was just before her ninetieth birthday. She wrote to me in Hong Kong, inviting me to the celebration, and was clearly a little peeved when I wrote back and said it would be difficult for me to make the ten-thousand mile journey for this occasion. She died in 1987, just before her ninety eighth birthday. Rest in peace, Aunt Elly, you leave many friends behind.

4

Music in Amsterdam During the War

The war meant for me, as for so many others, the start of a new life. In May 1940, the month of the German invasion, I had finished high school, and intended to enter university. The war also meant that international artists could no longer come to Holland, and concert life suffered terminally. My autograph collection therefore comes to an end in 1941. Also, I was slowly outgrowing this hobby and from the age of nineteen onwards, I was more interested in meeting and talking with artists than simply asking for their autograph. My other occupation, turning pages, also suffered from the same shortage of opportunities, but here another element entered the picture. A young man of my age during the war was always prone to run into an SS trap for forced labour, or worse, to be reported to the Germans by Dutch Nazi collaborators. While attending concerts and mixing with the crowd was probably as good a way as any to remain inconspicuous, it was quite another to put yourself on a concert platform to be seen by friend and foe.

I thought of closing these stories with the last of my autographs, but in some respects the war was also a continuation of the peace by other means for me. I do not intend to dwell on my wartime experiences – this is not the place for that – but I hope I may be forgiven for sharing one memory, which I have never forgotten. Shortly after the capitulation in May 1940, I was walking in the street with my father. It was an unseasonably hot day, but all around me I could see smoke coming out of chimneys. I asked my father what it could be at this time of year. His answer was clear and direct: Jewish people were burning valuable papers. This was a totally spontaneous action, but no doubt started by the many German refugees who knew from experience what lay ahead.

In September 1940 I entered the law faculty of Amsterdam University, and joined the students corp, for which a three-week hazing period was required. I had also joined 'Sweelinck', the Student Music Society. Normally I would have had to join the Dutch army in 1940 but with the war going on and the German occupation, this was no longer an option. In a way I was fortunate in being able to complete my first half way examination in 1942 before the Germans demanded of students a signed 'declaration of loyalty and no resistance to the occupying forces'. Ninety-five percent of the students refused. This coincided more or less with the barring of Jewish professors and students. A brave, non-Jewish, professor in the Law Faculty of Leiden University challenged this by calling a meeting in the large auditorium at which he gave an emotional speech of loyalty to one of his particularly famous Jewish colleagues and challenged all professors and students to boycott the university and refuse to sign the declaration of loyalty. This was tantamount to closing this oldest university of Holland, which was also one of the oldest in Europe. Needless to say this professor had to go into hiding at once. His name is worth recording: Professor Cleveringa. He survived the war and will be forever remembered in Holland.

A few months later Amsterdam University followed this example. This meant automatically that professors and students were assumed to be in breach of the decrees imposed by the Germans. Before closing, the professors let it be known that in faculties where independent study was possible, they were prepared to give students a work programme and a book list, and, more importantly, to take examinations in the privacy of their homes and give an informal passing note. I took advantage of that and in this way managed to complete my doctoral studies before liberation. My first duty, however, was of a different kind. I joined my many fellow students who went into the underground Resistance movement. As I said, this is not the place to relate my wartime experiences. Suffice it to say that they demanded all-out activity interspersed with long periods of inactivity.

This is where I would like to resume relating my musical activities. I always loved the sound of the clarinet and when it appeared that I might have some time on my hands, I approached the first clarinet of the Concertgebouw Orchestra, **Rudolf Gall,** and asked if he would take me on as a pupil. This was an immodest request because a musician of his stature would normally only take professional students or at least advanced amateurs, but this was wartime and he could use the money, so he accepted me. Rudolf Gall was a German who had been engaged by Mengelberg in the thirties because of his outstanding abilities. Mengelberg always demanded 'solo' tone, which Gall had in abundance. He was a kind and gentle man who lived with his family in a modest second-floor apartment, not far from the Concertgebouw. It was there that I appeared once a week for lessons. He also took the trouble to buy an A and B flat clarinet with me and to teach me how to fashion the reeds which came from France.

All went well until one day when coming to lesson I saw a Nazi swastika flag flying from one of his apartment windows. I went upstairs and asked him the reason for this. He was crestfallen and said: "You know, I have never been a Nazi, quite the contrary,

but all German orchestra members have been ordered to fly the flag on penalty of dismissal. I have a family and young children to support and cannot afford to lose this position. I told him that I was very sympathetic but that I could not in good conscience enter a house which flew the Nazi flag and so had to terminate my lessons. He understood and almost cried. I continued to hear him in the orchestra and meet him at the Concertgebouw. One of his memorable recordings was with Jo Vincent in Schubert's *Der Hirt auf dem Felsen* (The Shepherd on the Rocks). After the war I heard he had gone back to Germany, to the Bavarian Radio Orchestra, one of the best in the country. On one of my home leaves from the Far East, in the early sixties, I happened to be in Munich and tried to contact Gall. A colleague in the orchestra told me that he had committed suicide a few years previously. This, I think, was a true German tragedy. It happened at the same time as the joint suicide of the Nazi conductor Oswald Kabasta and his wife, also in Munich.

Another activity I took up was attending occasional orchestra rehearsals. I suggested earlier that a concert hall, either during a performance or a rehearsal was a relatively safe place to go unnoticed, and immune to raids. It had no doubt also something to do with the fact that the Nazi boss of Holland, the Austrian Seyss Inquart, was a keen music lover and encouraged active concert life as far as he could. This did not mean that he could or would prevent the Jewish members from being barred from Dutch orchestras. For some time they were allowed to form their own orchestra, which performed in a theatre in the Amsterdam ghetto and was only allowed to play music by Jewish composers to a Jewish audience. Its conductor, Albert van Raalte, a former conductor of the Radio Symphony Orchestra, where later Bernard Haitink fiddled, was a friend of my family. Permission to attend Concertgebouw Orchestra rehearsals was given to me by Willem Mengelberg.

At this time I started another hobby. With my pocket money I bought many miniature scores. They were surprisingly cheap in those days and over the years I acquired quite a collection which is still with me. One of the more memorable rehearsals I attended was by **Herbert von Karajan,** then General Musik Direktor of the Aachen Opera, just across the Dutch border. He was very young (in his early thirties) to be a General Musik Direktor, although in a minor position compared to the much older Wilhelm Furtwängler, Karl Böhm or Clemens Krauss. But his ego was already inflated by his membership in the Nazi party and the German Kulturkammer. He came to an old-established and world-renowned orchestra of an occupied country and he represented the enemy. Needless to say, there was a certain amount of resentment on the part of the orchestra which was not helped by some of Karajan's idiosyncracies. He already had the habit of closing his eyes when conducting and this the orchestra considered a mere mannerism. The critical part, however, came at a rehearsal of Brahms' 4th Symphony, at which I was present. He told the orchestra at the beginning of the first movement "I will raise my arms and you on your own will start the upbeat. I will come in on the next bar." This is visually and orally effective because in fact the sound would seem to be welling up of its own accord, allowing the conductor, as it were, to ride in on the wave of the main theme.

So he raised his arms and nothing happened. He repeated patiently his intention and went through the same motions. Again nothing happened. He then told the concertmaster that possibly the orchestra had not understood his German, which was in itself a bit of an insult to an international orchestra, and ordered him to explain the matter to the orchestra. Whereupon the concertmaster said, "Herr von Karajan" - not Maestro, mind you, which he thought was his due - "You are paid to conduct. We are paid to play. You conduct, we play." Von Karajan never came back to Amsterdam. Interestingly Svíatoslav Richter relates a story of rehearsing the Tschaikowski Concerto with von Karajan. After the cadenza in the second movement when the main theme returns he waited for von Karajan to give him the upbeat, which he had specifically requested. Von Karajan obstinately refused.

A more pleasant and more positive experience was the appointment of the German conductor Eugen Jochum (1902-1987) as first guest conductor from 1941 to 1943. Jochum was a sympathetic and first class musician. He was steeped in the German Bruckner tradition, which was anathema to Mengelberg and thus to the orchestra, although Mengelberg did conduct a few rare performances of some Bruckner symphonies in earlier years. Jochum had conducted Bruckner for the first time in 1926, when he was in his early twenties. Bruckner repays the effort of following the score during performance, as the entire architectural structure becomes visible on the page.

I made a point of sitting behind the orchestra in the amphitheatre during rehearsals, where I could see and hear the conductor talk to the orchestra. Tradition has it that orchestras expect a conductor to conduct and not talk too much. This is not always true. It was a revelation to see how the orchestra paid attention when Jochum took them through their paces in Bruckner. He was like an architect, carefully explaining the function of every stone for the greater glory of the entire cathedral. The orchestra responded in like manner and their performances became more informed and inspired by the day. It helped that Jochum was a patient teacher who could also listen. A contemporary conductor popular with the orchestra for the same reason is Nikolaus Harnoncourt.

I remember a particular innovation Jochum introduced in the final movement of Bruckner's 5th Symphony. This movement, and thus the symphony, climaxes in a massive chorale played by the brass, and supported by the entire orchestra. Jochum brought in double-brass players on the horn, trumpet and trombone, whom he called his 'twelve apostles'. He explained carefully that throughout the more than an hour-long symphony the brass played a prominent part and the players were therefore physically tired, or at least no longer fresh, at the beginning of the last movement. The doubling brass players would alternate during the first part of the movement, thereby giving other players an occasional respite. When the climax, i.e., the chorale, came, all the brass players, now refreshed, played together, making an overwhelming impression. He added, diplomatically, but sincerely, that this can only be done when the walls of strings are strong enough to support such a massive brass roof, and the Concertgebouw, he said, was just such an orchestra. Many years later I heard Christoph von Dohnányi conduct the same Bruckner symphony and afterwards I asked him what he thought of the idea of doubling the brass in the Chorale. His reply was cold and brief: "I don't tamper with the score." Far from tampering, Jochum did not change a single note or tempo, but only brought forth the essence of Bruckner in an artistically and entirely justified and convincing way. Bruckner would have approved.

Jochum had a pronounced anti-Nazi past and was later invited by the Concertgebouw to be Guest Conductor in 1958 and 1959. After conducting the traditional Beethoven cycle in 1960, he was appointed Principal Conductor jointly with Bernard Haitink the following year. He continued to conduct in Amsterdam as Guest Conductor until 1987, the year of his death.

Conducting seems to be a healthy profession. It is certainly a profession which provides sufficient physical exercise conducive to old age, if one is to think of people like Toscanini, Klemperer and Solti. I met Jochum for the last time in, I think, 1985, at the Bregenz Festival, where he was conducting the Bamberg Symphony Orchestra. We spoke about Japan, where I had heard him before, and he mentioned that he had been invited to do a tour with the orchestra which would include sixteen concerts and quite a bit of travel. He was already in his eighties and he had asked if he could bring a fellow conductor along with him. The Japanese, who were adamant about wanting to hear him, turned him down flatly. "We want to hear you," they said. "Alright, I am going alone," replied Jochum, and completed the arduous tour at an age when others would have long since retired.

Following scores in rehearsal and hearing conductors talk to the orchestra made me realise how inadequate the theoretical underpinning of my musical knowledge really was. I managed to insinuate myself into a theory class at the Amsterdam Conservatory and even took the first exam. I found later in life that a little knowledge can go a long way towards musical appreciation.

To those who get the impression that the war was for me a succession of concerts, attending rehearsals and music lessons, I would only say that as time went by and Holland became harder pressed and oppressed by the Germans, and finally went hungry, life and work in the underground movement became a hazardous occupation which eventually required a false identity and long periods away from home.

In 1942 the Germans established the Jewish ghetto, which was an extension of the original Amsterdam Jewish neighbourhood. All Jews of Amsterdam were gradually assembled here (rounded up would be a more accurate way of describing it), for easy transportation to the transit camp of Westerbork, with Auschwitz or one of the other death camps as their ultimate destination.

In the early days permission was given for the Jews in Amsterdam to form an orchestra, but they were only allowed to play the music of Jewish composers. Their concert venue was an old theatre in the ghetto, formerly the 'Hollandsche Schouwburg'. Albert van Raalte, formerly with the Radio Symphony Orchestra (which was definitely not the least of the Dutch provincial orchestras), was appointed as conductor. Van Raalte lived a block away from us, and visited my father from time to time. I remember that he came to see us the day after the orchestra's opening concert. He had tears in his eyes when he spoke of the performance of Mendelssohn's *Italian Symphony*, a work of purest joy. To this day I cannot hear the symphony without this memory coming back to me. The orchestra's existence lasted barely a year, due to the large turnover and eventual lack of players. Albert van Raalte later perished, and the old Jewish theatre subsequently became the collection point for all death camp transports. Van Raalte too was taken there.

Since the war so dramatically affected all aspects of life, I may be permitted to put down a few personal thoughts on the relationship of music to the private and public world in which we live. For me, the beginning of the war marked the conventional moment of coming of age and development of personality. In matters of musical appreciation, my page-turning had given me the opportunity to witness in close proximity the recreation of music by gifted artists. When that activity fell away and my university life was replaced by active underground work, alternating with study, it was inevitable that music would become either less or more important to me. It turned out to be the latter, and my passion for music was to last for the rest of my life.

In a sense, music is the purest human experience, as its enjoyment emanates from, but is not linked to a physical presence. It can be experienced without one being aware of the medium and the memory of music retains more of its essence than the diminishing perception of a painting, a play or a dance. I became aware of this when I realised how much music sustained me in my wartime underground activities, which, athough painfully real, occasionally took on an almost surreal quality. Music, on the other hand, was unalterable. I came to see that for performing artists music was the only real life, and that its physical aspects (whether they entailed hardship or enjoyment) were often ephemeral. At the same time I realized the need for music and for the image of it to be kept free from contamination. Always involuntary, contamination can take the form of the self-righteousness of a Furtwängler or the naiveté of a Mengelberg. Both these individuals were fully aware of the power of the music they recreated, since their main purpose was to articulate it. They cherished the illusion, however, that through their medium music could raise man above his material instincts in real life. They refused to see that 'their music' was daily abused for evil purposes. No punishment can do justice to this misconception or is really required, if only because the perpetrator has committed no worldly crime. But they realized, long after the event, that their lofty ideal of music had been prostituted through confrontation with the reality of life.

In his play *Taking Sides*, Ronald Harwood has Furtwängler finally collapse when confronted with the question "Have you ever seen a death camp like Auschwitz, the human furnaces, the pile and stench of corpses, the total abnegation of humanity?" What then becomes clear to Furtwängler in the play is that his heroic and superb performances of Beethoven's Fifth Symphony and the grandeur of Bruckner had been simply used to further the greater glory of Germany's conquest of the world. The huge swastika flag often suspended as backdrop behind the podium should have alerted him. This perversion of music perhaps reached its climax when, as mentioned earlier, the Germans in Amsterdam made a Jewish orchestra play for a Jewish audience, both of whom had been condemned to death. In that sense the war was for me a turning point: I came to see music as the only essentially unadulterated value in life. I hope readers will forgive this deviation from my promised story telling.

The end of the war came none too soon, in May 1945, when I was twenty-three years old. At this point, I again had the urge to end this book. But, looking back, this was also the time when the freedom of life was just opening up for me and the following fifty years provided some interesting and amusing experiences. Readers who came for the autographs therefore please stop here. Others kindly follow me.

5

After the War: Paris, Amsterdam, Hong Kong and Beyond

After the war, with my law degree in my pocket, I intended to sit for the entrance exam of the diplomatic service. But the Dutch government, just returned from London, was in no position or mood to deal with the niceties of diplomatic appointments. The home front naturally came first. I did call on the Secretary of State of the Ministry of Foreign Affairs, a distinguished senior diplomat called Snouck Hurgronje, who kindly received me and said "The first diplomatic exam is planned for the end of this year, or beginning of next year, but if you want to prepare yourself, pay particular attention to your knowledge of languages, French and English. This seemed sound advice which I took to heart. Since my French was much worse than my English I decided to spend some time in Paris after the summer holidays. Every Dutchman or Dutch woman needed a summer holiday in 1945 and I was no exception, not that there was anywhere to go. The tourist industry had not yet been reborn and there was of course no foreign exchange, but clean air and a bit of sun after the 'hunger winter' was all we needed. So in September, refreshed and reasonably well-fed, I went to Paris on my pocket money and a small sum from my father which he called a book allowance.

Paris in 1945 was of course not the glittering city we knew before the war, and were to know again much later, but it had much to offer. I took a small room in the student quarter of St. Germain-des-Prés and enrolled myself as one of four foreign students at the Ecole des Sciences Politiques, 'Sciences Po' for short, in the Rue Guillaume Trois, where the great and grey André Siegfried was still teaching. I had to get used to the custom that before sitting down in the student amphitheatre, you shook hands with all students around, whether you knew them or not, and again before leaving. Paris did not have much to offer except of course its rapidly and colloquially spoken French and I don't remember having gone to any concerts. Either there were none, or I had no money. I do remember, though, a marvellous performance by Madeleine Renaud in *La Folle de Chaillot*. Otherwise Paris was in the grip of the existentialism of Paul Sartre and Simone de Beauvoir, who had not yet written her famous *The Second Sex*, and a bit of left-over and warmed-up *Nouvelle Vague* of pre-war cinema. One evening I heard the chansonnier Charles Trenet, 'Le fou chantant' in an unforgettable programme of mostly his own songs. He died in February 2001.

I returned in December 1945, a little more confident in my French, which was after all the object of the exercise. I was informed by the Ministry of Foreign Affairs that in November a limited diplomatic entrance exam had taken place, which my friend Hugo Scheltema, later Ambassador to Jakarta and the United Nations in New York, had passed, and that another exam was scheduled for February 1946. Already a number of applicants had registered and I put my name down too. There was not much you could do to prepare yourself, except read the news in depth, if possible including foreign publications, and rely on your general knowledge and the impression you made on the examiners, drawn from the Ministry, universities, banking and business worlds.

With again some time on my hands, I restarted a semblance of student life (the student corps had suffered a good many war victims), and regularly went to the Club. I was accepted, or perhaps tolerated, although strictly speaking I was no longer a student, having formally graduated in May of that year by handing in the informal wartime passing notes given to me by my professors after the examinations at their home. However, there soon appeared an opportunity to be active. All corps societies had been revived, including Sweelinck, the music society. The first public performance after the war was organised to take place in 1946, which was also a lustrum year, so a gala occasion was planned in the large hall of the Concertgebouw. Knowing my interest in music, and the circumstances that I had more time on my hands than most active students, I was asked to take over the Presidency of the Society, and the responsibility of preparing the gala concert for the end of April 1946. I accepted, and had the good fortune of finding excellent fellow committee members, including girls, from the girls' student society, without whom I would not have been able to accomplish the task. This book includes a photograph of the Sweelinck committee, standing together with the members of the girls' student music society. It was taken in the 'hall of mirrors' in the Concertgebouw at the reception preceding the concert in 1946. It was our first concert to be held after the war. Third from the right is my friend Alexander Verrijn Stuart, quaestor (treasurer) of the society. Alexander made an illustrious career as Professor of Information Technology at the University of Leiden and also made a name for himself as leader of a Dutch Himalayan expedition. We have now remained friends for sixty years.

A young composer, also our conductor, Bertus van Lier, was commissioned to write a special work, and he appropriately composed a large cantata for choir and orchestra,

The Sweelinck Music
Society Committee.
The author is in the
centre.

based on songs written during the the 80-years War of Independence against Spain, around 1600, an appropriate work of thanksgiving for the liberation of Holland. The original collection of songs was attributed to Valerius, and called *Valerius - Gedencklank* (Valerius Memorial Song Book). This collection also contained Holland's national anthem of twelve verses, only one or two of which are normally sung. The concert was a great success, both, as the saying goes, publicly and critically, and took place in front of a full house. We had indeed managed to assemble a large orchestra and choir.

I had one small problem, however. Since the concert was announced as a gala occasion, white tie and tails were obligatory. Not only did I have to preside over a reception, I had to make the official speech. I did not own these garments, and the for-hire outlets were not yet well stocked. They would not have had my size anyway (I am six foot three). So as a last resort, I went to my friend Klaas Boon, the first desk viola player in the Concertgebouw Orchestra, who was my size. Klaas generously said, "This is my working dress. I have two sets. Feel free to borrow one!"

Before that concert, another event occurred. Like an aging film star, I made a belated come-back as page-turner on the 11 January 1946 at the ripe old age of twenty-four. It was a concert I shall always remember: **Benjamin Britten** (1913-1976) and **Peter Pears** (1910-1986) were giving their first concert in Holland after the war, and Britten had chosen this venue for the European premiere of his song cycle *The Seven Sonnets of*

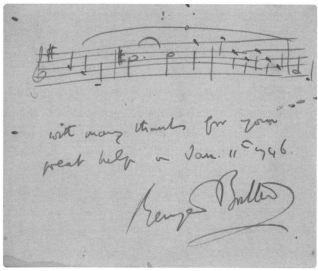

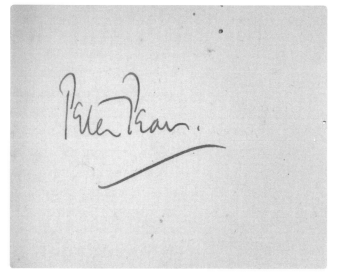

Michangelo. I had met Britten before, and he asked if I would turn pages for him, but he added that he preferred to play from the manuscript because it gave him the feeling of recreating the work while playing. He was a kind and considerate man and added that if I had difficulty in reading his handwriting in the manuscript, he would play from the printed score. I told him that if he could give me ten minutes with the score, I was sure I would manage. From experience I knew that composers make handwritten corrections in their manuscript or even paste loose strips of paper over a page. Britten's score was no exception. But his handwriting was clear and the concert went well. It became, as it were, the point of rehabilitation of Amsterdam's concert life. Britten wrote a gracious note in my autograph book, preceded by the first bars of the work they had just performed, with Peter Pears on the next page. In hindsight I consider this to be a suitable ending to my page-turning and autograph-collecting career.

Another event took place before the April Sweelinck concert, this time non-musical. In February I sat for my written and verbal entrance exams for the diplomatic service. I had reason to be grateful for the suggestion to brush up on my French and for my recent stay in Paris. All thirty candidates were asked to write a short essay on the American Federal Reserve banking system (the American Central bank), in French. I do not know how this particular effort was judged, but just before the April concert, I was informed that I and five other candidates had passed. I was summoned to the Ministry of Foreign Affairs and told by the Minister himself that my first post would be Bangkok, at that time not yet a Legation but a Military Mission, in view of the presence of 10,000 Dutch prisoners of war released from Japanese camps and now under allied protection. In November 1946 I left for my destination, a week after the King of Thailand was found dead (perhaps murdered) in his palace. This was Ananda, the older brother of the present King Phumipol.

I had two postings in Asia, the first in Bangkok, and the second in Batavia, which was not yet Jakarta at that time. I joined a small section of the Ministry of Foreign Affairs which was attached to the Governor General, and advised him in matters of foreign affairs. Timing was critical. Holland was carrying out what it called two 'police actions' (in effect a full-scale war) against Indonesian 'rebels', and once I had occasion to visit the front line. But again that is another story.

While the Diplomatic Service has many attractions - sometimes in agreeable, and always interesting surroundings - freedom of choice is not one of them. I longed for a profession where I could be more master of my own destiny. I therefore left the service after my second posting, grateful for the many things I had learned, and decided to join the international insurance business. Insurance law had been the optional subject for my doctorate. After several interludes, which I spent in Europe and America, I accepted an offer from one of the two largest re-insurance concerns in the world, the Swiss Re-Insurance Company of Switzerland, to manage their affairs in Asia. I was based in Hong Kong, with an office in Tokyo. Over the years I added offices in Manila and Singapore and served eleven Asian markets. Re-insurance requires a modicum of diplomacy, combined with technical skills and it suited me fine. I was Managing Director of the Swiss Re for twenty years, until my retirement at the age of sixty three. Although ready for retirement, I was then asked by a Swiss friend of mine, Hans Baer, Chairman of Bank Julius Baer, to open an office for the bank in Hong Kong and later in Tokyo, to serve their Asian markets. I will explain later briefly how this came about and how it affected my para-musical activities. I left the bank when I was seventy, and my wife and I retired to our homes in Switzerland and Spain from where we immerse ourselves from time to time in Europe's many musical offerings.

I have the feeling that those of you who have borne so long and patiently my little stories have become friends, and one needs friends to tell stories. If possible, please bear with me a little longer. I shall now tell my remaining stories which are strictly anecdotal and take place in different continents, where I happened to be working, or was travelling on business or vacation. I have led the international life I wanted and liked and in the process brought up an international family. I might say here that my wife is from Thailand, my children were raised in Hong Kong, America, Switzerland and England and we now live far apart, my wife and I in Europe, my daughter married in America, one son in Melbourne, who is a financial advisor, the other an architect in Singapore, both independent. I have family and many friends in Holland, but only go there to visit. While this background is not essential, it will explain the setting of some of the stories.

We arrived in Hong Kong on Christmas Eve 1958. Hong Kong today has a skyline which rivals New York, but in 1958 there was no building taller than five or six storeys, and all were in the colonial style of the nineteenth and early twentieth century. The two parts of the city, the island of Hong Kong and Kowloon on the mainland, were connected by ferry, which stopped at midnight, forcing the late-night traveller to take a little chug-chug boat called a sampan. Hong Kong in 1958 had a population of three million (to double in thirty years) and more than one million were refugees from mainland China, after the fall to Communism in 1949. The Hong Kong government, with a gigantic effort, managed to provide low-cost housing for these refugees, almost at the pace of their influx into the colony.

The success story of Hong Kong has repeatedly been told. Suffice it here to say that the recipe had three ingredients: a vast and cheap reservoir of Cantonese Chinese labour, the post-Communist influx of Chinese intelligentsia, with capital and entrepreneurial skills from Shanghai, and a dedicated policy of the Hong Kong government to pursue a total laissez-faire policy with regard to economic development, including a refusal to ask for outside help, and of course low taxation. Even today Hong Kong has no external debt. Milton Friedman, the Nobel prize-winning founder of the Chicago School of Economics, wrote of Hong Kong more than once as his ideal city-state. In another sense, Hong Kong was in the sixties and early seventies often called a cultural desert. It had no orchestra, no concert hall and no music school. Its talented youngsters went overseas to study and often did not return. Still, a city that can play host to the Berlin Philharmonic Orchestra under von Karajan, and the incomparable Amadeus String Quartet, albeit in a Chinese movie theatre, must have been an oasis in the desert.

For a long time Hong Kong was not a destination for performing artists, but a point of transit to Japan. All this changed in the seventies with the building of the new City Hall on the waterfront, including a concert hall, the founding of a professional symphony orchestra and a Centre for the Performing Arts which housed the Conservatory. My wife joined the Ladies Committee of the Hong Kong Philharmonic as soon it was set up, and even before that I took over the Chairmanship of the Hong Kong Chamber Music Society, which presented concerts of foreign and sometimes local chamber music groups. I found enough time to play the piano and clarinet and for twenty years sang in the local Bach choir. A Cultural Centre of international size and style was built up in the eighties, and this put Hong Kong definitely on the cultural map, where it still is.

Returning to my own story, in 1959 I took up a habit which has not left me since. I read every issue of *The New Yorker* magazine. Readers will question the significance of this but it led soon to one of my most treasured acquaintances. Then as now, *The New Yorker* was a magazine of the highest literary standards and a pioneer of what is now called investigative journalism. Essays could be short or published over a number of issues. In 1959 the serialisation of a book, later to be named *An Intimate Memoir of Sir Max Beerbohm*, by S. N. Behrman appeared in *The New Yorker*, and it at once caught my attention. Behrman had before the war been a very successful writer of society plays on Broadway. He was also a scriptwriter much sought-after by Hollywood. Max Beerbohm, of course, was the illustrious turn-of-the-century caricaturist and essayist who in 1899, at the age of twenty five, became the successor of Bernard Shaw as drama critic of the London *Saturday Evening Post*. Shaw gave him a name that stuck throughout his life: "the incomparable Max". Beerbohm, who was actually not fond of Shaw, whom he considered not an artist, but a social reformer, responded at once in print with "compare me." Any comparison was usually in his favour.

After the war, public taste had changed and Behrman lost his theatre audience. However he did not lose his writing skills and unusual choice of subjects. Sir Max Beerbohm (he was knighted in 1939) was a very private man, and had in 1910 retired to a house in Rapallo, in Italy, where he lived until his death in 1956, at the age of eighty two. He made frequent visits to London, where he lived during the war, and became famous for his BBC broadcasts on a variety of subjects. After the war, Beerbohm had done something most unusual for him. He rarely wrote letters but he had commented in writing to Behrman about something the latter had written. A correspondence developed that gave Behrman the idea of asking Beerbohm if he could visit him. Beerbohm at once agreed and from a long series of visits, over several years, in the fifties and a growing friendship, the idea came to Behrman to write "an intimate memoir of Max". Surprisingly, Beerbohm did again something he had never done before. He agreed. The book appeared in 1961, but before that the entire work was serialised in *The New Yorker* magazine in 1959.

In the meantime, Sir Max Beerbohm had died in 1956. If Beerbohm was a man of exquisite taste, brilliance and modesty, Behrman was an equally brilliant writer, with a touch of understatement which Beerbohm came to value highly. Behrman also had the natural fluency of style of a writer who had perfected his art for stage and screen. The series fascinated me from the beginning, and I could hardly await the next issue. Readers will know by now that I am not shy in approaching people whom I have learned genuinely to admire and respect, and so I wrote to Behrman, care of *The New Yorker*, about the impression his book had made on me. His response was not slow in arriving and in it he said that his fan mail, quite considerable in the 1930s, had been long a thing of the past, and he was delighted to receive a letter on a book of his that was certainly not written for the general public. In his letter, dated May 17, 1960, he said: "I am sixty-seven, and have met many people, but I never have encountered so exquisite a sensibility as Max's. It causes a kind of despair in me that there cannot be more people like him. I don't mean as an artist – that would be asking too much, but humanly speaking. And yet, when I get a letter like yours, I am encouraged."

A brief correspondence ensued, at the end of which he sent me an inscribed copy of his book and invited me to visit him in New York if I ever had occasion to do so. Unexpectedly, there did arise an opportunity in 1962, when I had to be for some time on business in Philadelphia. I wrote to Behrman and asked if I could visit. He wrote back and said yes, and suggested that I come first to his home, Park Avenue, corner of East 88th St, whence we would repair to his favourite restaurant, the Four Seasons, where he always had a table. I presented myself at the appointed hour at his very large apartment, where he lived with his wife, and he welcomed me with great warmth and charm, redolent of older times. He was an old gentleman with a great sense of humour. He asked me if I had time for a leisurely lunch. He himself, he said, was a man of considerable leisure and so started one of the most memorable short interludes of my life. He took me to the Four Seasons restaurant in the Seagram Building, which had been completed three years earlier (architect Philip Johnson), to show me the collection of Mark Rothko paintings. They had been specially commissioned for the restaurant.

I did not really know all that much about Behrman, even about his past fame, so I encouraged him to talk about himself. He was a quintessentially modest and retiring man, but he knew his worth. Someone later told me that before the war he was called 'Slippery Sam', but 'elusive' would have been a better way of putting it. It soon dawned on me that I was in the presence of a very special person. Almost in passing, he mentioned plays he had written for Alfred Lunt and Lynne Fontanne, Laurence Olivier and Noel Coward. He was a great friend of Greta Garbo, for whom he wrote the screenplays of *Queen Christina* and *Anna Karenina*. At that point he began to resemble for me Artur Rubinstein as a raconteur. But then he mentioned a film he made in 1944, which I had seen and liked tremendously – Yakobovsky and the Colonel, the virtuoso combination of comedy and drama as an adaptation of a work by Franz Werfel, with Danny Kaye and Kurt Jürgens in the main roles. It was a story of a German Jew, fleeing in 1940 from the Nazis, through France, and meeting up with a German colonel who used the Jew's wit to extricate both of them from extraordinary circumstances. It was at the same time the story of Franz Werfel and his wife Alma Maria Mahler, who fled Europe by the same route. When Behrman mentioned this, he interrupted himself, and said: "Do you know that Alma Mahler (Franz Werfel had died) lives here in New York? Since you tell me you love music, would you like to visit her?" I answered: "I would naturally be thrilled," and he said he would arrange a meeting over a weekend when I could come over from Philadelphia and he would let me know.

But Behrman was full of surprises. During our lunch, he said that Vladimir Horowitz, the pianist, was a good friend of his, to whom he used to give tickets to his plays and films. It so happened that Horowitz was giving a party for his, I believe, 59th birthday that very night. This was during his period of withdrawal from the concert platform, which ended in 1965. Behrman asked if I would like to come along. I could not believe my ears and could only say that I did not want to gate-crash. He said, "You would not be gate-crashing. Horowitz has no idea who is coming and I will explain to his wife Wanda" (who was the daughter of Toscanini). And so I went that night with the Behrmans to the party. Horowitz lived not far away in an equally large apartment. The place was full of celebrities, in fact wall-to-wall: Leonard Bernstein, Gregor Piatigorsky, the cellist. I was told that Heifetz was there but I did not see him, and I was delighted to meet up again with Artur Balsam, for whom I used to turn the pages twenty five years earlier when he accompanied Nathan Milstein. He was a short man, five-feet nothing, and I remember that he could barely span an octave. When playing octaves he had to play very rapid arpeggios! Balsam made a concert career as well, and at the time of our meeting was still a presence on the concert scene.

Horowitz walked around among his guests wearing his favourite bow tie of the day. When he came to me, and I was introduced to him, he said: "Ah, a member of my Dutch public! When did you hear me last? I played there in 1934." I had to reply that that was a bit before my time. "Whom did you hear then?" I decided to mention a fellow countryman of his, Alexander Brailowsky. Horowitz replied in that self-deprecating manner, which demanded a rebuttal "Ah, my friend, Brailowsky, a much better Chopin player than myself." He may well have been right. I remember listening to a Horowitz recording of a Chopin mazurka with a friend who knew Horowitz. "Why does he play it so fast?" I asked him. The laconic answer was, "He cannot play it any faster!"

Before moving on, and learning that I came from Asia, he asked if many pianists came to Asia. I could only say: "Too few, but when you gave your first concert in New York after many years of absence from the concert podium, your Japanese fans chartered a plane to come to New York."

I was particularly thrilled to meet there Rudolf Serkin, an exact contemporary of Horowitz, who had said of Serkin "I love him like a brother, but if I told him that I consider the fugue in Beethoven's Hammerklavier Sonata much too long, he would kill me." I had heard Serkin many times in concert. Temperamentally and artistically, he was the exact opposite of Horowitz. Can we imagine Serkin playing the Stars and Stripes with double octaves? He told me he lived on a large estate outside Vermont and one of his hobbies was to go round his estate driving an agricultural tractor. The whole party was as relaxed as Horowitz himself and I enjoyed every minute of it.

Shortly thereafter, Behrman telephoned me in Philadelphia with a date for a visit to Alma Mahler. But he added "You will have to go alone. Alma knows me too well and my presence might inhibit her. It will be up to you to separate fact from fiction." She lived in an apartment on a fairly high floor and it took me some time to get upstairs because the lift was out of order. I arrived somewhat out of breath, which is never a good pre-condition for a first meeting. She was a grand old lady, tall and unbent at eighty-three, but her legendary beauty had, of course, faded. Her apartment was comfortably old-fashioned. I told her that I had read her book *Memories of Gustav Mahler* and her autobiography *Mein Leben* and that was a cue for her to start reminiscing.

Even at eighty-three, she had a great sense of self-dramatisation, and I remembered what Behrman had said about separating fact from fiction. I did not have the heart to ask her about her romance with Gustav Klimt, the most famous painter of Austria at that time, when he was thirty-five and she was seventeen. In her autobiography she claimed that he was head over heels in love with her and even followed her to Venice, where she was holidaying with her family. They had to meet in the crowd in St Mark's Square! But shortly thereafter, when she was about eighteen, she discovered her composition talents and became a pupil of Alexander von Zemlinsky, already a well-known composer and brother-in-law of Arnold Schoenberg. I asked her if it was true that she had one day asked Zemlinsky for the score of one of his quartets and the blunt reply was "you wouldn't be able to read it; you have talent but little ability." What she did not say was that she had told her mother at about the same time that she was going to marry Zemlinsky. She was then about nineteen. She did not know Mahler until she was twenty-one, and they got married within half a year of their meeting.

I asked her why she stopped composing, for which she had indeed a real talent (she had written a good many songs), and she replied: "Mahler told me there could not be two composers in a marriage and I then decided to devote my life henceforth to making my husband happy. I think I did that." Again I skipped her well-known adultery with Gropius, which is documented in the anguished annotations in the score of Mahler's 10th unfinished symphony. "You know what it means," he wrote at the end of the Purgatorio movement, referring, of course, to her affair with Gropius. I also did not refer to her three-year passionate relationship with Kokoshka, who wrote her pitiful letters in 1915 from the Front, when she, without telling him, was already living with Werfel. When Alma broke off the relationship Kokoschka was heartbroken and fashioned himself a life-sized doll resembling Alma, which sat on the sofa of his living room. To Franz Werfel Alma did stick through thick and thin (witness their perilous escape from Europe in 1940 through occupied France).

She was a curious mixture of naiveté and savoir vivre. Yet there is no doubt that she inspired men like Klimt, Zemlinsky, Mahler, Gropius, Kokoshka and Werfel, all artists of enduring and extraordinary power, above all creative. There were many who wondered what people saw in her, and the answer is probably that they saw what they wanted to see. And in that respect Alma was always very co-operative. She then soliloquized a bit about the scandal-ridden performances in Vienna of Arthur Schnitzler's *Reigen* (the play which inspired first the film *La Ronde* in the 1960s, and now Stanley Kubrick's *Eyes Wide Shut*). Of course she was well acquainted with Arthur Schnitzler and his daughter, who later committed suicide.

We concluded on a happy and truthful note: a discussion of the Mahler Festival organized by Mengelberg in Amsterdam in 1920, which she attended from beginning to end. She had known Mengelberg since her marriage to Mahler in 1901 and she confirmed how close the two men were. When asked whether Mahler would perhaps listen to suggestions by Mengelberg about instrumentation, she replied "without a doubt." Mahler had the greatest respect for Mengelberg as a conductor and that is worth remembering when we judge him today.

Although much of what Alma Mahler told me can be found in her memoirs, the meeting was nevertheless one that I shall not forget. She died in 1965 at the age of eighty-five.

Back to Hong Kong. Of the public concerts, I remember Jimmy Loughran with the Hal-lé Orchestra and that marvellous pianist John Lill. Jimmy gave me some of his recordings, which I still have. Another artist we looked after was Neville Marriner, who became a friend. He came with his own orchestra of St Martin in the Fields and after Hong Kong we met in Salzburg, Zürich and elsewhere. Though quite famous and probably the most recorded conductor in the world, a record he might share with Sir Georg Solti, he is still in my view somewhat underrated internationally. He ought to be in front of a major orchestra.

A light-hearted interlude was the visit of Nigel Kennedy, the gifted young English violinist who came with the recommendation and blessing of Yehudi Menuhin. Nigel Kennedy was what we would now call a cross-over artist in that he played classical and jazz music with equal love and fervour. Incidentally, Menuhin in his time was also a bit of a cross-over artist, although not in the same spontaneous way or as brilliant as Nigel. Readers will remember Menuhin playing and recording with the jazz violinist Stéphane Grappelli (of the 'Hot Club de France') and with the sitar player Ravi Shankar. Nigel came to Hong Kong either just before or just after his 'punk' period. In any case, he was normally dressed and coiffed, but he did not wear white or black tie in concert. I was asked to look after him, which I did with pleasure. He was young and ebullient, and also unconventional, as this story will show. After a magnificent classical performance with the Hong Kong orchestra, he asked me rather shyly (as though he was not sure what my reaction would be) if there was any jazz being played in town. Knowing his speciality, there was no point in taking him to a nightclub with a twenty-piece band, so I said: "There is a hole in the wall in Kowloon where three ageing Australians play jazz, improvising in Dixieland style. But the place is badly lit, smoky and rather grubby." "Fine" said Nigel, "we are on our way."

The place consisted of two narrow buildings, one of which contained the bar. By literally going through a hole in the wall one entered an adjoining building where a small stage had been built for the three Australians, who conducted nightly jam sessions. They did not care about their appearance, usually sported a three-day-old stubble, and only stopped for drinks. Nigel and I took a seat at a table against the wall, and I could see at once that he was enjoying himself. After fifteen minutes he could no longer restrain himself and picked up his violin case (remember this was after his concert, so he had to carry his instrument with him). If the three jazz players were surprised they did not show it. They nodded to Nigel, whom they did not know, of course, and waited for what was to come. Nigel, as a true performer, simply tuned up his instrument and started to play. Not a word had been exchanged. The pianist fell in at once, and so did the other two, one on trumpet and one on double-bass. It was a fascinating performance - true improvisations on a tune everyone knew, and it indeed sounded like a St. Louis band. Each musician did his solo, then another took over, except that Nigel was perhaps the greater virtuoso. Suffice it to say that I got Nigel back to his hotel very late (or rather early in the morning), and he asked if he could go again the following night, but a bit earlier, say at ten. I was delighted to indulge him in his marvellous playfulness and readily agreed to take him. I should mention that he brought his young wife to Hong Kong, but she did not come to the jam sessions.

The next night he did not get back to the hotel until three o'clock in the morning, and at ten I received a phone call from the orchestra manager telling me that there was a rehearsal, and that Nigel had not turned up. I rang his room, and was told that he was still asleep. I forget what excuse I made, but the rehearsal was postponed until the afternoon. This would not have been possible with the players of any other orchestra, who would simply have refused to play outside 'union' hours. Instead of Nigel, it was me who was severely reprimanded, for not taking better care of my ward. In fairness to Nigel, he did not repeat the outing again, which only the two of us (and I suppose his wife) knew about, and when he was saying goodbye, he told me with a wink that he had enjoyed his visit to Hong Kong much more than to any other place. The orchestra management was duly pleased, and so was I...

During the time that I lived in Hong Kong, I used to have to travel frequently on business, much of the time to Japan. For the para-musical side of my life this was fortunate, because although Hong Kong had become a centre for the arts in its own right, it was still something of a cultural desert in comparison with Japan. In every respect Japan is in Asia but not of Asia. Japan has a separate and distinct culture. It has never been colonised, embraced Western civilisation eagerly a mere hundred years ago, had a large and fully developed economy along Western lines. Not that the Japanese had lost their own individuality – they are one of the most homogeneous people in the world, and in many ways are quite self-contained. To realise this, one has only to attend a Noh performance, Kabuki show, or their marvellous puppet theatre Bunraku, which I came to like tremendously and rarely missed.

The Japanese have deep pockets, both individually but especially institutionally, as far as Western art is concerned, particularly music and painting, Their private museums are treasure houses of Western art, acquired with corporate money. They are very eclectic and therefore often not large. In an hour you have seen the Bridgestone Museum with its choice of Impressionists, or the collection of the Fuji, formerly Yasuda Insurance company, whose chairman I knew professionally. The latter paid the highest amount for a Van Gogh painting, some $76 million dollars. Never mind that during the recession he had to sell it at almost half the price and that it is now back in America. Another way of lifting the tip of the veil of the Japanese character is to experience an old-fashioned dinner party, complete with song, dance and geishas and its exquisitely prepared and presented food. This was my good fortune in the sixties and seventies, when visits of foreigners were less frequent and therefore more celebrated. They are also vastly expensive, another reason why your Japanese host today will invite you to a good restaurant instead. This by way of introduction to my non-professional experiences in Japan.

There are several great orchestras in Tokyo, Osaka and Nagoya, in which the string sections are especially noteworthy - think of the now internationally famous Suzuki method of teaching the violin. Their high standard is often ensured by long annual visits of foreign conductors. For years I was able to hear Kurt Masur and Horst Stein for part of the season and Western guest conductors are frequent, not least because of the generous honoraria. When I mentioned earlier deep pockets, any Western orchestra that wanted to make a tour of Japan was warmly welcomed and paid for by industrial or financial corporations. The Berlin Philharmonic with von Karajan, Vienna with Josef Krips, and later Lorin Maazel, the Concertgebouw with Haitink, the New York Philharmonic with Bernstein and the Chicago Symphony with Solti and Barenboim. In fact, not rarely could one hear more than one such orchestra within one week. Another attraction for foreign orchestras and conductors were the many large and acoustically fine concert halls. Foreign architects and acoustic specialists were often employed. Two examples of extreme Japanese extravagance. When Horowitz came out of his self-imposed retirement, his Japanese fans chartered a jumbo jet to visit New York. Another: in the seventies the entire Metropolitan Opera was invited and financially sponsored for a series of performances which included their own singers, orchestra, chorus, sets, stagehands and a generous appendage of hangers-on. I happened to be in Tokyo, and went to see *Fidelio* with an American friend Richard Silverman, who had lived for many years in Tokyo and spoke fluent Japanese, with a perfect Brooklyn accent,.

Richard was an ardent opera fan and spent most of his waking hours in or around the Met during their Tokyo visit. After the performance, Richard took me to see the star of the performance, Beverly Sills, who is still remembered as a great and versatile artist, and as an outstanding coloratura. After her retirement, sensibly at the height of her career, she managed hands-on for many years the New York City Opera and even today she is still active on the New York scene as Chairman of the Lincoln Center. When she received us, she said, looking at Richard, "You know, we both come from New York, and have the same surname, Silverman, but for me, on stage, Silverman is such a mouthful that I changed it to Sills." And still looking at Richard, she said: "By the way, Richard, where do you live in New York?" When Richard said "I actually live here in Tokyo," she looked quite surprised and said "I thought you were part of the troupe." She then ordered coffee for the three of us and we sat and talked for a long time. To me she remarked, "Opera is so early here that it is over well before my bed time, and I need to talk to unwind." I was so lucky that she chose that night to unwind in Richard's and my company. On a different level, I also saw in Tokyo the show of the American musical *Hello Dolly!* with the original cast, headed by Ethel Merman. Here I did not go backstage, although the performance was memorable.

In the early nineteen seventies in Tokyo I heard Daniel Barenboim, who was then barely thirty years old. He was performing with the English Chamber Orchestra whom he conducted from the keyboard. I sat on the balcony of the large Tokyo Bunka Kaikan Hall and suddenly spotted Barenboim's wife Jacqueline du Pré playing among the celli. After the concert I went backstage to compliment and thank Barenboim, and I told him how much pleasure he was giving me with his recordings of all the Mozart piano concertos (also with the English Chamber Orchestra). When I asked him how he found time to perform this herculean task amongst all his other commitments, Jackie interrupted from the other side of the room where she was packing up her cello: "He never practises!" I replied that in that case he was in good company, since Arthur Rubinstein had always said that practising was a bad habit. Never at a loss for repartee, Jackie said, "Daniel never told me that!" Barenboim asked me which concerto I had bought and my answer was: "I first bought the *Coronation*, but having heard it I had to subscribe to them all." The project was not finished until 1975. At that point the room had filled with well-wishers and autograph hunters, and Jackie and I decided to let Daniel have the limelight to himself. She had not been recognised by anyone, and while she was waiting for Daniel to finish, we sat on a sofa and talked. As is well known, Jackie was a very lively girl, who was full of laughter and she never stopped talking. She was somewhat puzzled by my presence in Tokyo, and by the fact that I lived in Hong Kong. In her view foreigners lived in Europe and America, but there were only Japanese people living in Tokyo and only Chinese people in Hong Kong. I tried to turn the conversation back to her, but she said "No, everyone talks about me. Let's talk about you." So, against my inclination, I found myself talking about my past and present, and before I realised it I was deep into my autograph collection and all the page turning I did before the war. She seemed fascinated by this Dutchman's odd hobbies, and interrupted frequently with questions. In the end I managed to get back to her. I told her that over the course of my many years of association with musicians I had long ago stopped doing something that artists detest: flattering them. But I could not help telling her, in all sincerity, that as a cellist I considered her in a class with Casals and Rostropovich, with no one else coming even near. This was the first moment in which she became pensive and said, "That is very kind. You didn't have to say that." But being Jackie, she could not help adding: "Surely you didn't come to that conclusion tonight, when you saw me among the celli!" When we parted company she said "Please come and visit us in London and bring your autograph books." When years later, I was in a position to do so, it was too late. Jackie was gone. I have not seen the film recently made about her private life, and I do not think I will. It seems irrelevant to her great art. She is sorely missed. I did not see Barenboim again until more than fifteen years later, in Hong Kong.

Let me tell you of another meeting in Tokyo I shall never forget. I had bought a ticket for a concert of the renowned Russian pianist Sviatoslav Richter and the excellent NHK Orchestra. It was a full house and everyone was there for the concert to begin except Richter. After twenty minutes the impresario appeared on the platform and we expected the worst. But he only said "Mr Richter is alive and well, but delayed in traffic and will be here in twenty minutes." This became thirty minutes and throughout you could hear a pin drop, so quiet was the audience. Eventually he appeared amid loud applause. He played two concertos that night – Mozart before and Beethoven after the intermission.

As always, Richter's almost mystic concentration was a unique experience, and I do not use that word lightly. For me, the striking moment was the cadenza in the Mozart concerto K432 in E flat. It was inordinately long, too long in fact, but of such unusual beauty that in the intermission I could not resist going backstage. I did not want to go after the concert, when the Japanese literally besiege their artists for autographs.

I found the door of the artists' room open, and peering inside I saw Richter alone in shirtsleeves. "Do come in," he said, "nobody talks to me." After introducing myself and thanking him, I said "I came for a special reason. Who was the composer of the cadenza? You yourself?" He smiled and said "No. Not by me, but come and see for yourself." The score was open on the table and Richter approached it as a man with a well-kept secret. I looked at the manuscript and the notes leapt out at me. Richter saw my surprise and asked "Do you know by any chance whose it is?" And he could not believe his ears when I said "This is Benjamin Britten." I then told him that twenty-five years before I had had Britten's handwriting in front of me for two hours, when I turned pages for him and therefore could not help recognising his script. He looked delighted and slightly deflated when he said "I thought I was the only person in this house who knew Britten."

He then started reminiscing how at Britten's own festival at Aldeburgh they used to play Mozart's Sonata for Two Pianos K448. It was later recorded. He added that Britten had a greater affinity with Mozart than he himself. He actually said he preferred Haydn, which in hs later years he played, indeed, more often than Mozart. In the course of our conversation, which lasted the whole intermission, he said: "I normally don't like playing in big cities, but the Japanese are such private people and equally allow one one's privacy that I make an exception for Tokyo." Towards the end he said "You must come to my own brief festival in Tours, France." I made a mental note of this and by good fortune was indeed able to go the next year.

The festival endured for many years. The venue for the concert I attended was a small baroque gem of a theatre and I took my daughter along, who was that year studying in Paris. That season we heard Rostrpovitch and Fischer-Dieskau, both in partnership with Richter, and Richter in recital alone. The Fischer-Dieskau/Richter partnership produced one of the most memorable concerts I have ever heard, Fischer-Dieskau's love for the clearly spoken text spurring Richter to greater expressiveness and articulation. After the concert Richter seemed pleased to see me and Rostropovich, whom I had met earlier in Hong Kong, gave me his bear hug reserved for friends. These are the sort of memories I think worth sharing with you.

For a period Richter and Rostropvich were very close, not only giving concerts together, but also going to a masked ball as two crocodiles entering the door on all fours, and other parties where Rostropovitch played a balalaika decked out in a long false beard and gold pince-nez. Later they drifted apart, for all kinds of reasons. In

Sviatoslav Richter, the most exceptional pianist of our time and also an exceptional human being.

Richter's own words: "He always took credit for everything and harboured intentions that had nothing to do with music." However it could also have been a typical Russian trait of two artists of near genius being too close for their own good.

Going back to that Tokyo concert, when I was about to take my leave from Richter, he said: "Incidentally, I was not stuck in traffic tonight. I got into a taxi and went to the Tokyo Bunka Kaikan Hall, where I always play, only to find it in total darkness. Suddenly I remembered that the concert was in the brand new Suntory (of whisky fame) Hall, but my imprerssario found that too fanciful an explanation." I heard him again in a recital in Nagoya, where I sat very near the podium. I remember being struck by the fact that Richter had very large hands which could span a twelfth. He played the last chord of the Schuman Toccata without arpeggiation, a feat I have never heard before or since. As a curiosity, Josef Hoffman - whom I never heard - had very small hands; he could barely span an octave. Steinway built him a special piano with a keyboard made to measure, so that he could play a ninth. I heard Richter for the last time towards the end of his career in 1992 in the Festival Hall in London. He long ago had started to play with the hall in total darkness and one spotlight trained on the keyboard, the score in front of him and his glasses half-way down his nose. I found this sight of Richter a slightly unnerving experience. Myra Hess in her last year also put the score of works she had played by heart all her life in front of her. In her case it was failing memory. In Bruno Monsaigeon's book on Richter the pianist himself gives the true reason for playing from the score. As he grew older he found that his perfect pitch had deserted him. He would start playing in A minor and hear it in B minor. So in an attempt to correct it he transposed what he was playing with the result that, without intending it, he would land up in G minor. In his own words: "This is extremely inconvenient, especially if I am playing with an orchestra. Following an absolutely frightful concert in Tours, when I played eight of Lizst's Transcendental Studies and a recital in Japan, where I took fright even before launching into Beethoven's op 106 Sonata, I made up my mind never to play again without a score." This was the frank explanation he gave to Monsaigeon. To the press he said: "It is a more sincere way of playing: you can see all the marks the composer put in the score and execute them more faithfully." A final idiosyncracy: he disliked choosing a piano. "You tend to regret your choice during the concert. Play on any piano, but practise on the best. It is extraordinary how much time pianists will devote to their choice of a piano bench, sometimes hardly looking at the piano." Sviatoslav Richter had only the best. A prophet in his own country: around 1980 a question went around the Moscow Conservatory: "When will Richter go out of fashion?"

Once again I am returning to Hong Kong and now come to an event which led to three lasting friendships and which eventually changed the course of my professional life, although the event itself was purely musical. I refer to the visit of the Zürich Tonhalle Orchestra to Hong Kong in 1981. Tonhalle is the name of the concert hall in which the orchesta performs, as in the 'Concertgebouw' in Amsterdam. Both buildings happen to have been built around the same time, more than a hundred years ago, and boast excellent acoustics.

The Tonhalle Orchestra is one of the major European orchestras and its first visit to Hong Kong was therefore an event of some significance. I represented a large Swiss company, based in Zürich, the Swiss Reinsurance Company – Swiss Re for short. Like most of the other large Swiss companies and banks represented in Hong Kong it was an important patron of the Orchestra in its hometown and therefore no large-scale entertainment was planned by branch offices in Hong Kong. I felt, however, that the visit could not pass entirely unnoticed and my wife and I decided to offer a Chinese banquet to a cross-section of the orchestra and the accompanying Board members and guests. The latter included a ninety year-old former mayor of Zürich.

The visiting party was presided over by the Chairman of the Board of the Tonhalle, Hans J. Baer and his charming wife Ilse. Hans Baer is a great and generous music lover and both he and the eponymous bank of which he was Chairman are substantial patrons of the orchestra. In addition, Hans of course had to devote a considerable part of his time and influence to the affairs of the Tonhalle. At the dinner party I said a few words of welcome, to which Hans graciously responded. The first friendship link was thus forged that night and strengthened on my subsequent visits to Zürich when I was repeatedly a guest at their beautiful home, often after a concert, with conductor and soloist present. I and my wife came highly to treasure this friendship with him and his wife Ilse. Sadly, Ilse has since passed away. A few years later Hans remarked to me that he had learned that I was reaching retirement age at Swiss Re, and he asked if I would be prepared to stay on for a few years in Hong Kong to open an office for Bank Baer and later perhaps in Tokyo. I welcomed a change of professional activity and accepted. In 1985, after a global trip to the bank's offices, I started in Hong Kong as Senior Representative of Bank Baer.

Knowing my love for music and interest in musicians, Hans had said "Occasionally I have artist friends who go to Hong Kong and know no one there. May I ask you to extend a welcome to them?" This he later called the Baer-Brouwer hospitality. I was, of course, more than happy to oblige. The first agreeable surprise came when he announced that Sir Georg Solti was coming to Hong Kong for the first time with the Chicago Symphony Orchestra. Solti had arrived in Switzerland in the early war years as a gifted but penniless Hungarian pianist. He later won the piano competition in Geneva and had been received and supported throughout the war by the Baer family. Hans was therefore one of his oldest friends.

Solti's meteoric career is sufficiently well known not to need repeating here. He and his lovely wife Valerie were going to spend a week in Hong Kong, where the Chicago Symphony were to give several concerts and I felt privileged to be asked to look after them. At that time Solti knew no one in Hong Kong. Apart from the obligatory sightseeing, which in Hong Kong is always a thankful exercise, I took Solti, who had a marvellous old-world charm and warmth, to the Hong Kong Conservatory, where we happened to walk into a room where a Chinese girl was practising Chinese music. Solti listened with fascination and after a while joined the girl on the piano stool. He said to the girl (she understood English) "Do you know that some of the intervals you play remind me of Hungarian music?" He started to play some Bartók for her and both the girl and I were greatly surprised to hear distant similarities.

I had a good Chinese friend in Hong Kong, a medical doctor P. P. Chiu, who had a passion for Western music and loved to entertain visiting musicians in his hospitable home. He was a well-to-do man and had built a large home on a mountain side overlooking the South China sea. From the terrace you could see the sun set exactly

between two mountain peaks across the bay, something that had been meticulously planned by P. P. (the terrace not the sunset). This was quite spectacular. In his home he had a large music room with a grand piano where he organised chamber music concerts. His brother, P. W. Chiu, who looked after the family fortune, was an accomplished violinist who often played there. P.P. and P. W. and their wives Bella and Margaret were inseparable. After the war, P. P., who had studied before the war medicine in England, taught himself French, German and a bit of Italian, and was therefore able to make most foreign visitors feel at home. His Chinese cook was famous in Hong Kong and P. P. entertained in the lavish style to which Chinese food is so suited. The large round table, which seated more than twelve people, had a polished lid in front of each guest, below which there was a tube for chicken and fish bones and the like. I have never seen this contraption elsewhere. After dinner we would move to a large rectangular table where fruit and tea or coffee were served. P. P. had a curious habit, of which we had to apprise our guests. When he entertained foreign guests he never ate himself. He always said, "One cannot entertain properly and eat at the same time." I forgot to mention that P.P. also had on display a valuable collection of ancient Chinese copper vessels. When I mentioned to P.P. Solti's forthcoming visit, he asked me at once to reserve a night for him. The Soltis were happy to accept and the reader can imagine that the evening was memorable indeed. Chinese banquets also lend themselves to extended conversation between courses. For years afterwards Solti would mention this, for him, unique evening.

Solti and I spent many hours together and one morning he walked into my office unexpectedly, sat down and said "This is a good time and place for me to learn something of international finance. Can you tell me what derivatives are?" I was somewhat taken aback by this unexpected demand. I told my secretary to hold all calls and launched into a subject on which I was by no means an expert. Fortunately Solti was even less so. At the end of the morning, he said, "I know, you want to talk about music. But we can do that on my home ground. You are hereby cordially invited to visit me in London." We did so in fact regularly.

I remember several dinner parties with a large number of non-musical celebrities, but the music talk he had in mind came when he invited me to spend an afternoon with him when he was free. I had remembered one of Solti's habits. He was a man of tremendous energy, both on and off the platform, but after a concert he was understandably physically tired and received visitors sitting down. Valerie would always bring him one whisky and soda which would pick him up at once. So that afternoon, I brought him a gift box of a bottle of aged single malt whisky and several miniature bottles of different vintages. When receiving it he looked at his watch - it was 2.30pm – and said "It is a bit early, but shall we try it?" And so we did. By then we had been friends for a number of years and he allowed me to call him Gyuri. Valerie left us alone - she is no whisky drinker – and Solti started to show me his basement where all the walls were hung with Prix de Disques certificates. He proudly announced that he had more than any living artist, classical or otherwise. Incidentally, the official spelling of his name, Georg without an "e", is the German one, because he went to Germany first after the war. Returning to the basement, the other item of note was an immense grand piano, at least a metre longer than a concert grand. He had found it in Italy where a crazy pianist had commissioned it to be built for himself. Solti could not resist buying this curiosity. When after a long afternoon of his and some of my recollections, many of his related in his autobiography, I took my leave. Valerie showed me to the door and said "I'm very upset. I didn't get a minute to talk to you, so I am going to invite you and Mon (my wife) to lunch at the Savoy tomorrow and Gyuri is not invited."

At the end of Solti's Hong Kong visit he gave a supper party for the entire Chicago orchestra, plus wives, board members and attendants. This is customary after a long overseas tour and in this case included almost one hundred and fifty people. He did it at the Mandarin Hotel, where he stayed. He mixed freely with the guests, but had dinner at his own table, where he asked us to join him, and which he shared with some personal friends and Daniel Barenboim, who had been selected as his designated successor, and who had come to Hong Kong to conduct the last concert. I was pleased to meet Barenboim again after Tokyo, twenty years before. Jackie of course had died and both Barenboim and myself were older and greyer.

My most recent memory of Baremboim was the closing concert he gave in Seville in the summer of 2002 with his West-East Divan orchestra, made up of young Jewish and Arab musicians (18 to 25 years old). The initiative for this venture had been taken jointly with Edward Said, a Palestinian by birth, and professor of comparative literature at Columbia University. The first year they met in Weimar (Goethe's town, hence the name West-East Divan). Barenboim was that summer conducting in Bayreuth and motored in the morning to Weimar to rehearse with the orchestra. In the afternoon he returned to Bayreuth to conduct a five-hour Wagner opera and the next day would repeat this pattern. The meeting in Seville had been sponsored by the Spanish *Society of the Three Religions* (Jewish, Muslim and Christian) and was a moving event. Each desk had a Jewish and Arab player and the first desk changed players at every piece. Mozart's concerto for three pianos was played: Barenboim in the middle with on either side a young Jewish and Arab pianist. After the concert he turned to the audience and said a few words in perfect Spanish (he was born in the Argentine). He closed by saying: "As an encore we will play the overture to *The Barber of Seville*." When after the concert I went back stage to congratulate him and tried to arrange a private meeting he said he had to fly back to Berlin the next day to conduct. Barenboim remains an amazingly talented and versatile musician.

Whenever I travelled I heard and saw Solti, in Zürich, Luzern and Salzburg. After von Karajan's death, when Solti conducted in Salzburg in July or August, he usually rented the home of the Belgian Consul General, a little outside Salzburg where he invited his friends to lunch in the garden. Here he was totally relaxed and always told a few jokes. Right after the war he rehearsed the Bavarian Symphony Orchestra, on an extremely cold winter day. The hall was still badly heated and the players kept their coats on. During a trombone passage, Solti reminded the first trombone that a note he played should be a third higher. The answer was "Sorry Maestro, I can't bend my arm enough with my coat on." The other story he liked to tell is better known, of Jessye Norman, a large lady, who was desperately trying to squeeze from stage right through a narrow passage to stage left without success. A helpful stagehand suggested "Why don't you try sideways?" whereupon Jessye's curt remark was "I have no sideways."

Now my last Solti story. After a Salzburg performance of Verdi's *Un Ballo in Maschera*, I made my way backstage and bumped into Placido Domingo. He said "You are a good friend of Solti's. Tomorrow is the annual football match between two festival sides. Do you think I could ask Solti to kick off?" I told him, "Of course. But I have another idea. There is always a small and rather poor brass band playing before the match. Ask Solti to conduct the band for one piece." So it happened, with great hilarity. Incidentally, Domingo once said in an interview that when he was young he seriously hesitated between becoming a professional football player or an opera singer. We are all grateful football lost out.

Solti died suddenly at Cap D'Antibes in the South of France in August 1997. He was on his way to Turin, with the Tonhalle Orchestra, when he suffered a heart attack. This was on the Monday after Princess Diana died in the Paris car accident. Solti was taken to intensive care but recovered quickly enough to be moved to a ward. When he was told of the Princess' death he decided to dedicate Verdi's *Requiem* which he was to conduct in London the following week to her memory, and told his London manager this over the phone. Two days later a second heart attack felled him and the *Requiem* was performed in the joint memory of Diana and Solti. As Valerie said, until the last, old age had completely passed Gyurgi by. At eighty-three he was as active as a man of fifty three. A last word in honour of Valerie. She is a lovely person, in every sense - and I do not use that word lightly - and in her own right, and as an essential support for her husband who could not have achieved what he did without her constant presence. I am happy that we continue our friendship with Valerie.

The story of my third friendship I will try to make a bit shorter. Again, the introduction to **Isaac Stern** came from Hans Baer. He too had been an old friend. Stern came to Hong Kong to give a concert and my wife and I looked after him and his wife Vera in Baer-Brouwer fashion. The second time he wrote he was coming for a few days rest before a tour of Japan. It so happened that a fundraising dinner had been planned for the Asian Cultural Council, of which my wife was a member. Stern was asked to be our guest of honour and say a few words after the dinner. He agreed at once. In fact, after arrival, he said "I've spoken as much for my supper as I have played for it." He gave his after-dinner speech in a very relaxed manner and told some of his innumerable stories, ending with an appeal for the Hong Kong Philharmonic. I am sure our guests dug deeper into their pockets after Isaac's appealing performance. This cemented our friendship and we kept up an irregular correspondence.

The third time we met we were already living in retirement in our Spanish home on the Costa del Sol. Isaac wrote that he was coming to Seville for a concert in a new modern concert hall, the Maestranza. He was bringing the Férenc Liszt Chamber Orchestra from Budapest and would as usual play and conduct himself. He wondered how far away we were, and whether we could possibly come and join him. We would have come from any distance, but it happened to be less than two hours. We were met

in Seville at the beautiful 1920s Hotel Alfonso XIII by Stern's impresario from Madrid, Mrs Keller, and had lunch with her. In the evening (concerts in Spain do not start before nine o'clock) we met Isaac at the new concert hall at Maestranza, as usual full of pep. He played and conducted a full programme. Afterwards we had dinner in a special restaurant we knew and at which Mrs Keller joined us.

It was already quite late when we returned to the hotel. The ladies retired and Isaac and I bought a bottle of wine and sat down in the beautiful Spanish-tiled patio, surrounding the inner courtyard, and started to talk. Isaac was happy and relaxed and we found much to talk about. He still had his spectacles shoved on top of his head, as was his habit. We are exactly the same age and therefore have the same span of memories, he from his elevated position, I from a more pedestrian one. He spoke of his struggle to save Carnegie Hall in New York, which he did together with the Chairman of the World Bank, Jim Wolfensohn, incidentally a distinguished amateur cellist. Just then they were seeing light at the end of the financial tunnel. I recalled turning pages for Bronislaw Huberman's pianist and seeing Huberman's time and accident-scarred face transformed into a beautiful mask. I could not help mentioning that in other ways Isaac resembled Huberman. Huberman was the founder and soul of the Palestine Orchestra, later the Israel Philharmonic, of which Isaac was the heart and soul. Isaac remarked that he had met Huberman only once, but that he considered him one of the greatest violinists of this century. Huberman would have liked that judgement, coming from a man like Isaac Stern. We agreed that one of the few benefits of old age is to have old memories, and to share them. On that, we ordered another bottle of wine. Isaac moved on the next day and my wife and I returned to Sotogrande. I was reviewing this book before going to press when the news reached me of the death of Isaac Stern in New York at the age of eighty-one on 22 September 2001. Isaac Stern's death marks the end of an era – not the era of superb violinists, for fortunately we have many of them. It marks the end of the era of 'engaged' musicians, that is to say musicians engaged in broad cultural, social and even political causes. Our talks in Seville touched on two of these, and I might just add Isaac Stern's well-known movie *From Mao to Mozart*, which he followed up with scholarships. I remember a chance meeting in Tokyo, when he had just returned from a trip to China. "I found yet another talented child," he told me. "She is coming with me to New York."

Isaac's predilection for young people not only showed itself towards budding performers, but also in his choice of chamber music partners. On one visit to Hong Kong, many years ago, he was accompanied by Emmanuel Ax at the piano and Yo-Yo Ma, the cellist, both in the early years of their careers.

The difference between Isaac and other performing musicians who support (mostly musical) causes was that with Isaac the personal effort came first, the money later. The image Isaac leaves behind, which I think he would have preferred, is not just of a great violinist, but of a man of his time with human interests. There were a few other musicians in the twentieth century who were similarly engaged on the cultural or political level, and who acted during their lifetime (it is easy to leave money in a will). First of all springs to mind Pablo Casals' total dedication to the struggle for a Spain free of Franco, which he put into words and deeds, not to mention music. A contemporary of Casals, Arturo Toscanini, steadfastly refused to conduct in fascist Italy and Nazi Germany and Austria. He was one of the main initiators of Salzburg's alternative festival in Lucerne, Switzerland, which is still going strong at the beginning of the twenty-first century.

A more recent champion of cultural and political causes was the violinist Henryk Szeryng, whose support of Poland and honorary ambassadorship of Mexico are well remembered. He died before he could achieve all he set out to do. A great musician of commitment, still with us, is Daniel Barenboim, with his earlier mentioned peace-making efforts between Israelis and Palestinians (the people, not the countries) and his fearless introduction of Wagner in Israel, the country whose passport he holds.

I am coming slowly to the end of my stories. We revisit Hong Kong and Asia almost every year. After all we have friends there of more than thirty years standing and if any proof were needed, Hong Kong shows it has long ago lost its label of cultural desert. In recent years we have heard among others Anne-Sofie Mutter and Itzhak Perlman there in recital. When I went backstage after Perlman's recital, I found the door to the artists' room blocked by hundreds of autograph hunters. I was thinking of the days long ago when I was practically alone, and not outside but inside the door. Perlman's charming accompanist, Miss Guggenheim, was standing guard outside the door on this occasion. We came to talk and she said that she was a friend of Itzhak's and lived on the West Coast (Itzhak Perlman lives in New York), and only played with him on tour. "But," she said, "You have not come to talk to me. Let me take you to Yitzhak."

Perlman was sitting somewhat forlornly in the room with his manager. He said: "Sit down and talk to me. I can't yet face the horde of autograph hunters." He then said something which touched me: "I must apologise for playing that rather cheap piece, *La Ronde des Lutins*." The latter is a 19th-century piece of pyrotechnics by a composer and great violinist called Bazzini, whose title means 'Dance of the Imps'. Yitzhak continued: "I couldn't put this piece on any programme in America or Europe, but I love playing it." I said: "Don't worry, you are in good company. Both Menuhin and Heifetz played it as one of their favourite encores and you are no less a violinist than these two." He answered "I'm glad to know. Let the young people in, I'm now ready to face them. After all, it was mostly for their benefit that I played that piece." When I parted from Perlman, he was signing numerous autographs. I mentioned that when President Truman had finished his memoirs, he autographed four thousand copies of them in one day. He even kept time – eight to ten per minute. Just as Britten was a fitting end to my autograph collection, at the age of twenty-four, so I think this is a suitable ending to my meetings with musicians at the age of eighty-one.

Readers might get the impression that at times I live and wander about in a ghost house, visiting now empty rooms. Nothing is farther from the truth. I live in the here and now. I treasure my large collection of CDs and LP records, some replays of 78 shellacs. But I have stopped comparing. One does not compare performances of fifty or more years ago with today's. One compares impressions of concerts, and these are highly personal and possibly biased towards the past, which after all form one's musical culture. There are exceptions though. In my collection appear autographs of three well known pre-war string quartets. I in fact heard six of the most famous ones, including the Budapest, the Kolisch, the Hungarian, and after the war, the incomparable Amadeus. But when I go today to a concert of the Alban Berg Quartet, I must say it is superior to anything I have heard in the past. Also, pianists like Andras Schiff, Murray Perahia and Mitsuko Uchida of the younger generation are comparable to the best of the past in a contemporary setting. Nor is my commingling confined to dead artists. I have a happy personal relationship with living artists, retired or performing, including Elly Ameling, Bernard Haitink, Mitsuko Uchida, Peter Schreier, Andras Schiff, Neville Marriner and Imogen Cooper to name a few.

Our concert going is now concentrated on selected festivals. Where else can one hear top performances in a short space of time? We have been going to Salzburg on and off

for forty years. We made friends locally which always gives us a sense of homecoming. But also, where does one find a festival management that asks two pianists of the stature of Alfred Brendel and Maurizio Pollini to play identical programmes, the last three Beethoven sonatas, within one week, for listeners to judge? Do not ask me to compare. And where else in the space of one week can one hear Mahler's 2nd Symphony with the Israel Philharmonic under Zubin Mehta, the 5th from the Concertgebouw under Bernard Haitink and the 6th from the Berlin Philharmonic under Claudio Abbado? Salzburg and the Schubertiade hold other special memories. For several years I would at least have one lunch with the tenor Peter Schreier and his wife and we would talk about anything from football and their sons to living in Dresden (then in East Germany) but travelling the world. One day he asked me if I had a wish for an encore. That night the encore was Schubert's *Der Musensohn* and I felt like an audience of one. Other festivals we have come to love are Glyndebourne, The Schubertiade at Feldkirch (now at Schwarzenbach) in Austria, Aix-en-Provence, Verona and the Rossini Festival in Pesaro.

Perhaps it is appropriate to end these memoirs with a recollection of one of my favourite artists, **Elly Ameling**, who is still very much with us today and remembered with love, although her voice can no longer be heard in concert. Elly Ameling ended her professional career a few years ago at the height of her powers, having delighted audiences all over the world for more than thirty years. Her chosen field was a specialized one, but not narrow: lieder and oratorios. It is interesting to note (especially for Dutch readers) that she followed in the footsteps of previous Dutch singers: Aaltje Noordewier-Reddingius (1868-1949), Julia Culp (1881-1970) and Jo Vincent (1898-1989), who in another age would have been world-famous. None of them ventured into opera, simply because there was no opera in Holland. Elly Ameling's argument was that her voice was not suitable for the opera house. Herein lies a certain modesty, another virtue of Elly's. The Mozart opera arias performed on concert podia were usually inserts or substitutes written by Mozart for particular singers and I could well have imagined Elly on the opera stage in a Mozart role. She has a lively personality which would have gone well with that composer.

I had the privilege of meeting Elly in the early 1990s, towards the end of her career, when she visited Hong Kong and my wife and I played host to her. We have since kept in touch, which is not an easy thing bearing in mind that she is constantly on the road giving master classes all over the world. A small anecdote may illustrate how successful she is in that field. Some years ago I had lunch in Salzburg with Sylvia McNair, a young but already famous soprano at the Metropolitan Opera. In Salzburg she sang Pamina in *The Magic Flute*. When she found out I was Dutch she said: "The largest single influence on my musical career has been the master class I took with Elly Ameling." This is the field where Elly is today in great demand, leading master classes all over the world, from New York to Tokyo.

It is always difficult to find a proper ending to a book, even when you have said all you set out to say. When in doubt the best solution is just to end it, which I now do.

Index of Principal Names

Numerals in bold refer to autographs and/or photographs.